THE BREAD BOOK

*the text of this book is printed
on 100% recycled paper*

THE
BREAD BOOK

Carlson Wade

BARNES & NOBLE BOOKS

A DIVISION OF HARPER & ROW, PUBLISHERS

New York, Evanston, San Francisco, London

First BARNES & NOBLE BOOKS edition published 1974.

STANDARD BOOK NUMBER: 06-463383-7

Contents

Introduction

The aroma of freshly baked bread is an old-fashioned memory of the past that can become the excitement of the present. Making bread at home yields satisfactions that can more than justify the time and energy expended in its preparation.

Home-made bread is always the best. It is freshly baked by yourself, using the ingredients that you select to satisfy your personal taste and good eating pleasure. Home-baked bread will offer you such rewards as the enthusiastic appreciation of your family, the personal joy of knowing you have created a symbol of goodness, warmth and security (since long before Biblical times) and the knowledge that the bread is a treasure of those essential nutrients needed by the family. It is the most exciting food that you can prepare for those you love.

Today, with modern methods, along with a variety of packaged ingredients, you can make a good loaf of bread with much ease and simplicity. You have a wide variety of different ingredients that are available to suit every budget, every time schedule and every taste bud. From the simple but delicious wheat bread, said to have been made some 10,000 years ago, we can today enjoy such favorites as fruit-flavored breads, sweet rolls and muffins, endless varieties of biscuits, waffles, pancakes, not to mention no-knead breads, quick breads, herb-flavored breads, wine-flavored breads as well as festive breads for all occasions.

Just a few small recipe changes and a simple loaf of bread becomes transformed into a joyous loaf of good eating. All this is possible because of the dedicated efforts of culinary artists of

5

the world, throughout the many hundreds of centuries, right
up to our present time.

Now, the art of cuisine breadbaking can be performed right
in your own kitchen, using simple equipment, with ingredients
available at almost all food stores.

The purpose of this book is to introduce you to the pleasures
of easy breadbaking . . . and the joys of good bread eating for
yourself and your family. The instructions are clear and simple.
The kitchen-tested recipes are gathered from all corners of the
world, to offer you a wide variety of taste treats to make your
home a happy, contented symbol of love and good healthy eating.

This book will show you how to make luscious loaves of
bread and related baked products and enjoy the old-fashioned
taste of home-baked foods. It's easy. It's good. It's just wonder-
ful!

THE BREAD BOOK

1

Breadbaking at Home

Breadbaking is surprisingly simple once you know the basics of preparation. Let's see how you can learn these breadbaking basics with this set of tips.

ALL ABOUT YOUR INGREDIENTS

To make sure that your home-baked bread has a delectable taste, perfect texture and beautiful appearance, ingredients that go into it *must* be the best. Each ingredient adds something to the finished product so each one has to be properly used. Let's get acquainted with your ingredients.

FLOUR

Flour isn't 'just flour'. It's the most important ingredient in home baking—the framework of almost every food you bake. *Wheat flour* is used to make bread because it has a protein called *gluten*. When flour is stirred and kneaded with liquid, the gluten stretches to form the elastic framework that holds the gas bubbles formed by the yeast. This makes the structure and elasticity of the batters and doughs and the structure of your loaf. The term 'flour' when used in recipes is understood to mean wheat flour unless otherwise indicated.

Different types of flour available are:

All-Purpose Flour Also known as 'general purpose' or 'family flour' it may be used satisfactorily for most recipes. This is flour milled from selected high protein wheats. The baking properties of choice wheats, blended carefully at the mills, should yield flour that will give you best results for everything you bake—from a wine-flavored festival bread to a fruit-flavored muffin.

Self-Rising Flour A convenience product made from all-purpose flour to which leavening and salt have been added in controlled amounts at the mill. One cup of self-rising flour contains the equivalent of $1\frac{1}{2}$ teaspoons of baking powder and $\frac{1}{2}$ teaspoon of salt. *Note*: Whenever you use self-rising flour for a standard recipe, *omit* the baking powder and salt since these have been added at the mill.

Whole Wheat Flour Also known as 'Graham flour', it is a coarse textured flour ground from the entire wheat kernel. It has a distinctive, nut-like flavor and color which is often associated with old-fashioned baking.

Rye Flour A finely ground product from the endosperm of the rye kernel, obtained by sifting the rye meal. Since rye flour does not form much gluten, it yields baked goods with a low volume.

Rye Graham Flour A coarse textured flour ground from the entire rye kernel. Like rye flour, rye Graham flour lacks gluten-forming protein and will yield baked products with a low volume.

Buckwheat Flour A finely ground product obtained by sifting buckwheat meal and offers a flavorful richness that makes the bread taste like 'old-fashioned' goodness.

Rice Flour A product milled from white rice. It is particularly useful for folks who have allergies to some grains. Rice flour can be used as a thickening agent or as flour in many baked products, including pancakes.

Soy Flour This is highly flavored. It is combined with wheat flour in baked products because it is low in gluten-forming substances. *Full-fat soy flour* is made by grinding soybeans that have only the hull removed. *Low-fat soy flour* is made from the press cake after all or nearly all of the oil is taken out of the soybeans. Soybeans may be heat-treated or conditioned with steam prior to oil extraction.

Corn Meal A species of grass, like wheat, available in flour form. Variations below. *Undegerminated Corn Meal* is ground from whole corn or from the endosperm of corn including the germ. *Degerminated Corn Meal* has the germ removed to obtain a more stable product with a longer shelf-life. *Bolted Corn Meal* identifies a product which has been sieved or sifted to remove the bran from the granular meal of the endosperm; it is ground finer than other corn meal. *Self-Rising Corn Meal* has varying granulation, from fine to coarse or 'straight' (with some flour as well as coarse particles in the mixture), to which the leavening and salt have been added. *Note*: As in self-rising flour, the leavening in self-rising corn meal represents the equivalent of $1\frac{1}{2}$ teaspoons of baking powder and $\frac{1}{2}$ teaspoon of salt to each cup of meal. Whenever using self-rising corn meal, omit baking powder and salt from the recipe.

Cake Flour is flour milled from low protein wheats and is specially treated and more finely ground than all-purpose flour. It is snowy white, starchy, soft and fine and produces cakes of large volume and melting quality.

FLOUR TERMS

The flour bag usually contains a complete description of the flour inside. The term 'flour' when used in recipes is understood to mean wheat flour unless otherwise indicated. When unqualified as to special purpose or preparation (as bread, self-rising), it means all-purpose or general-purpose flour. Here is what such terms mean:

All-purpose, general-purpose flour May be used for most recipes.

Enriched flour   Iron and the B complex vitamins (thiamine, niacin and riboflavin) which are removed during milling are returned to the flour by a process known as enrichment.

Organic, natural flour   The flour is neither bleached nor enriched and it contains all the natural ingredients as provided by the organic (non-chemical) soil upon which it grows.

Stone-ground flour   A milling method in which the kernels of grain are crushed coarsely between heavy, slowly rotating millstones much like those used by pioneers.

Instant, instantised, instant-blending or quick-mixing flour   A granular all-purpose flour that blends more rapidly with liquid than does regular flour.

Supersifted flour   A free-running flour which does not clump and minimises the tendency for a mixture to become lumpy. Specially prepared by suitable sifting techniques of milling.

HOW TO KEEP YOUR FLOUR FRESH

Flour can lose or gain moisture—a characteristic which can affect the amount of flour used in a recipe. To keep your flour fresh, keep it in a clean, airtight container and stored in a cool, dry place.

In humid weather, extra moisture in the air can cause unusually soft, sticky doughs. To adjust for a soft dough, *add more flour*— a little at a time—until the dough returns to normal.

Flour can be frozen for long-term storage if carefully wrapped in moisture-proof material. Freezing is especially helpful for dark flours which contain the oil-rich germ of the wheat kernel than can become rancid if improperly stored.

HOW TO SIFT YOUR FLOUR

Sifting loosens and separates the flour particles. Obtain a flour sifter or a nylon mesh basket from the housewares appliance section of any department store. It can last a lifetime.

HOW TO MEASURE YOUR FLOUR

To measure sifted or unsifted white flour, spoon tablespoons of the flour lightly into a standard measuring cup until the flour overflows the cup, or use a measuring jar or weighing scales. Do *not* pack the flour by shaking the cup or hitting with a spoon. Level the flour with the straight edge of a spatula or knife.

To measure whole-grain flours, instant flour, and meals, stir lightly with a fork or spoon but do not sift. Then measure according to directions for white flour given above.

A spoonful of flour makes the difference A cup of unsifted flour contains about 1 tablespoon more flour than a cup of 'home' sifted flour. For best baking results without sifting, this extra 1 tablespoon of flour must be removed. Here's an easy, accurate 3-step way to measure flour without sifting:

1. Spoon flour from bag or canister into measuring cup for dry ingredients (don't scoop or dip cup into bag). Fill to overflowing without packing flour into cup.
2. Level cup with straight-edge spatula. Remove 1 tablespoon.
3. Stir flour and remaining dry ingredients together with spoon or electric mixer at low speed. Leavenings and spices blend beautifully this way.

About pre-sifted flour Your guide is the package identification that this flour has already been sifted. It means that the miller has pre-sifted the flour before it was packaged, saving you the job.

LEAVENING

A leavening agent is one that causes the batter or dough to rise, increase in volume or bulk, and become light and porous during preparation and subsequent heating. Two basic leavening agents are used: baking powders and sodas and also yeast. Here's how to use them:

Baking powders and sodas: 'Mixtures of substances that liberate carbon dioxide in the batter or dough during the heating (baking) process.' There are two types of baking powder used in America: single acting baking powder referred to in this book as baking powder, and double acting baking powder.

To store: Keep tightly covered in a dry place. *To measure:* First stir the product to lighten it and break up any lumps. For best results, use standard measuring spoons and be sure the spoon is dry when the product is measured.

Yeast Yeast makes the dough rise and the bread light. It is a living plant that thrives on the sugar in the dough, producing the gas that makes yeast doughs and batters rise. Yeast also gives them a delicious flavor and aroma. Two types of yeast are available:

Compressed or fresh yeast available in cubes or cakes. It is perishable and should be stored in the refrigerator, where it will keep for at least a week. It may be kept in your freezer, wrapped in air and moisture proof wrapping, for several months, but must be defrosted at room temperature and then used immediately, with no delays or thought of refreezing. (For this reason it is best frozen in quantities which will be used at one time.) To use compressed or fresh yeast it is best dissolved in a cup of liquid. Cold liquid may be used but warm liquid (about 105–115°F) gives faster results.

Active dry yeast is similar to compressed yeast except that the yeast has been dried and is then packaged in granular form. Packed in individual, airtight packages or cans it will stay fresh on any cool shelf for up to six months and will give excellent results. (An expiration date is given on the back of the package.)

Active dry yeast may be mixed with the dry ingredients of the recipe or it may be dissolved in a cup of liquid about 105–115°F. *Alternatively*, the dried yeast may be mixed with a third of the flour in the recipe, all the liquid and a teaspoon of sugar and allowed to stand until the mixture froths (about 30 minutes) before adding the remainder of the ingredients—this is known as the 'batter method'.

LIQUID
The usual liquids used for making breads and rolls are milk, water, fruit juice and water in which potatoes have been cooked. Fresh whole or skim milk, reconstituted dry milk and evaporated milk all give good results. Milk should first be scalded for best results, unless it has been pasteurised or sterilised.

SUGAR
Sugar is the food the yeast needs to make the gas (carbon dioxide) which causes the dough or batter to rise. It also helps the crust to brown and adds flavor. Often, molasses, brown sugar or honey can be used effectively as a substitute.

SALT
Salt controls the action of the yeast, slowing the rising time. It also adds and brings out flavor. Salt substitutes and kelp (sea salt) may be used as effective replacements.

SHORTENING
Shortenings may be margarine, butter, lard, salad or cooking oils, or packaged shortenings created for baking. They help make the interior of breads soft and tender, increase the volume and add to the browning of the crust. Shortenings help give breads a much-desired soft, silky crumb and delay staling.

EGGS
Eggs add flavor and improve the structure so that breads can be richer and more nutritious. They also add color, help make the crumb fine and the crust tender. Eggs are often added to the dough to give the extra richness and golden color desired.

GUIDE FOR BAKING AT HIGH ALTITUDES
Barometric pressure declines with altitude. This may alter your finished baking product since the boiling point of water drops almost 2°F with every rise of 1,000ft in eleva-

tion. The higher the elevation, the lower the temperature of boiling water, and the lower the temperature within a baking product. Here is a guide:

Adjustment	3,000ft	5,000ft	7,000ft
Reduce baking powder For each teaspoon, decrease	⅛ teaspoon	⅛–¼ teaspoon	¼ teaspoon
Reduce sugar For each cup, decrease	0–1 table-spoon	0–2 table-spoons	1–3 table-spoons
Increase liquid For each cup, add	1–2 table-spoons	2–4 table-spoons	3–4 table-spoons

NOTE: For high altitude baking, it is usually necessary only to decrease your leavening and sugar and increase your liquid. Since every recipe is different and every location is different, only repeated experiments with each recipe can give you the most successful proportion to use.

BEFORE YOU BEGIN BAKING

1. *Read your recipe thoroughly.* Check to be sure you have all the necessary ingredients and utensils on hand.

2. *Assemble all ingredients and utensils.* Ingredients should be at room temperature for best blending, unless otherwise specified.

3. *Preheat oven to specified temperature for 10 to 15 minutes.* Incorrect oven temperature is often the cause of poor baking results. Be sure to leave room for the heat to go around the pans. When baking two loaves, place them on a centre shelf with 2in between them; if four loaves are being baked, put them on two shelves.

OVEN TEMPERATURE SCALE

(°F)
225
250
275
300
325
350
375
400
425
450
475

4. *Use baking pans recommended in recipe.* Correct pan size is important for best results. Measure the inside dimensions at the top if the size is not marked on the pan.

PAN SIZES

9 × 5 × 3in bread/loaf pan	10in pie pan
7½ × 3¾ × 2¼in loaf pan	1 quart casserole
8½ × 4½ × 2½in loaf pan	1½ quart casserole
8 × 8 × 2in pan	2 quart casserole
2½in muffin pans, cups *or*	Ring mold (6 cup size)
custard cups	10in baking pan

Although you can make bread with a minimum of utensils, you will get the best results with standard measuring and weighing equipment.

5. *Follow the recipe instructions and measure ingredients carefully.* The recipes in this book have been carefully developed so you can enjoy best baking results.

Standard American measures are given for each recipe.

All measures used in this book are level measures.

LIQUID MEASURES

The pint is 16fl oz. The ½ pint standard measuring cup is equivalent to 8fl oz.

HOW TO MEASURE YOUR INGREDIENTS
USING STANDARD MEASURES

Dry ingredients . . . spoon into nested or standard dry measuring cup until overflowing. Level with straight-edge spatula.

Sugar, shortening . . . press firmly into nested or standard dry measuring cup. Level with straight-edge spatula.

Baking powders, soda, salt, spices . . . fill standard measuring spoon to overflowing. Level with straight-edge spatula.

Liquid ingredients . . . place standard liquid measuring cup (8fl oz) on level surface. Fill to specified mark and check measurement at eye level. Use standard measuring spoons for small amounts.

HOW TO JUDGE QUALITY OF YOUR BAKED
GOODS

When is *done*? When the baking time is up, remove a loaf and tap the bottom or sides. It is done if it sounds hollow. Also, the appearance and crust should be evenly rounded with no bulges or bumps. The color should be uniform with no light or dark streaks. When cut, the crumb should be soft to the touch. The aroma should be pleasant. The flavor is tasty and soothing.

HOW TO STORE YOUR BAKED GOODS

Your home-baked muffins, biscuits, and unyeasted breads will stay fresh and moist if you wrap them tightly in aluminium foil, plastic wrap or an airtight plastic bag. Seal them well and place them in a cool, dry place or a bread box. Home-baked yeast breads and rolls store best in a polythene bag with the end loosely folded under so that some air can circulate and prevent the crust from becoming leathery. Baked goods may also be kept in the refrigerator if wrapped well. Refrigeration retards mould. Breads will become a little firmer in texture but food value does not change. Breads that have been in the refrigerator can be freshened up by wrapping in aluminium foil and placing in a moderate oven for 10 to 12 minutes. Serve quickly.

TIP: to avoid mould in hot weather, wrap the bread tightly in wax paper and store in the refrigerator.

A home freezer is the ideal place to store all baked goods. tightly wrapped and sealed in aluminium foil or polythene bags. Defrost at room temperature. Breads can be freshened up by wrapping in aluminium foil and heating in a moderate oven as above.

HOW TO KNEAD DOUGH

This should be done on a board or flat surface (a table or counter top) that has a little flour on it. Begin by rubbing some flour on your hands. Next—(1) Form the dough into a round ball. (2) Fold it towards you. (3) Using heels of your hands, push dough away with a rolling motion. (4) Turn dough one quarter turn around. Repeat until the dough is smooth and elastic, about 8 to 10 minutes. If dough becomes sticky, sprinkle the board with flour under the dough and rub more flour on your hands. (5) The dough has been kneaded enough when it is smooth, elastic and springs back when pressed with your finger. Thorough kneading gives uniform grain, fine texture and good volume.

NOTE: If you have an electric mixer with a dough hook follow manufacturer's instructions for using the dough hook to knead the dough. In general kneading time can be reduced to 2 to 3 minutes.

ALTERNATIVES TO PACKAGE MIXES WHEN THESE ARE UNOBTAINABLE
Packaged Biscuit Mix and Packaged Baking Mix

(1) Packaged scone mix. NOTE: As this is sweetened it may only be used in place of packaged biscuit mix in recipes which also require sugar or honey. The sugar or honey in the recipe should be reduced by 1 tablespoon for each 4oz of biscuit mix used.

(2) Home-made biscuit mix—use recipe for Home-Spun Biscuits on p 51, omitting the milk. Large quantities of this may be prepared and stored in a sealed polythene bag in a refrigerator for 2–3 weeks.

Baking Powder Biscuit Mix

Alternatives as (1) and (2) above.

All-Purpose Buttermilk Biscuit Mix

Home-made biscuit mix—use recipe for Buttermilk Biscuits on p 53, omitting the buttermilk. Large quantities of this may be prepared and stored as for home-made biscuit mix.

Orange Muffin Mix

Packaged scone mix is made up in the following way:

2 pkts scone mix
Rind of 1 large orange
2 eggs, beaten
¼ pint orange juice.

Put scone mix and orange rind into a bowl. Add the eggs and orange juice and mix well. Use as directed in recipe.

Pancake Mix

Home-made pancake mix

4oz plain flour
1 teaspoon baking powder
¼ teaspoon salt
2 tablespoons skimmed milk powder.

Sift all the ingredients together and store in a sealed polythene bag until required.

Packaged Hot Roll Mix (14½oz)

Home-made hot roll mix

Dry ingredients:

1½lb plain flour
½oz salt
¼oz sugar
½oz lard, rubbed in.

Yeast and liquid:

½oz fresh yeast dissolved in 14fl oz water
or

2 teaspoons dried yeast, 2 teaspoons sugar and 14fl oz warm (110°F) water. Dissolve sugar in water, sprinkle on dried yeast and leave until frothy—10 minutes.

Add yeast liquid to dry ingredients and work to a firm dough. Turn out and knead for 10 minutes. Cover and let rise until double in size, about 1 hour in a warm place. Use as directed in recipe. One package of hot roll mix is equivalent to half the quantity of recipe given on this page.

2

Basic Breads

Old-fashioned, home-baked bread was truly the staff of life. It offered a rich treasure of nutrients, filled the house with a delicious aroma, and made a slice of bread a delicious feast of good eating. With the flour available today, you can enjoy a wide variety of different basic breads to suit every taste and time schedule.

Coolrise White Bread (One-Bowl Method)

All-purpose sifted flour	5½–6 cups
Active dry yeast	2 packages
Sugar	2 tablespoons
Salt	1 tablespoon
Softened margarine	¼ cup
Warm tap water	1¼ cups
Cooking oil	

Spoon flour into measuring cup and level off. Pour on to wax paper. Now combine 2 cups flour, *undissolved* yeast, sugar and salt in large bowl. Stir well to blend. Add margarine. Add warm tap water. Beat with electric mixer at medium speed for 2 minutes. Scrape bowl occasionally. Add 1 cup more flour. Beat with electric mixer at high speed for 1 minute or until thick and elastic. Gradually stir in just enough of remaining flour with wooden spoon to make a soft dough which leaves sides of bowl. Turn out on to floured board.

Knead 5 to 10 minutes or until dough is smooth and elastic.

Cover with plastic wrap, then a towel. Let rest 20 minutes on board. Punch down. Divide dough in half. Shape into loaves: roll or flatten each piece into an oblong the same width as tin. Roll up like a jelly roll or fold into three; seal the ends. Place in greased $8\frac{1}{2} \times 4\frac{1}{2} \times 2\frac{1}{2}$in bread pans. Brush dough lightly with oil. Cover pans loosely with plastic wrap. Refrigerate 2 to 24 hours to rise. When risen to double the original volume and ready to bake, remove from refrigerator. Uncover. Let stand 10 minutes while preheating oven. Puncture any surface bubbles carefully just before baking. Bake at 400°F (hot oven) for 30 to 40 minutes or until done. Remove from pans immediately. Brush top crust with margarine if desired. Cool on racks. YIELD: 2 loaves.

Cornbread

Sifted flour	$\frac{1}{3}$ cup
Yellow cornmeal	$\frac{3}{4}$ cup
Baking powder	$1\frac{1}{2}$ teaspoons
Sugar	1 tablespoon
Salt	$\frac{1}{2}$ teaspoon
Eggs, beaten	1
Milk	$\frac{2}{3}$ cup
Melted shortening or oil	2 tablespoons

Sift together the flour, cornmeal, baking powder, sugar and salt. Combine the egg, milk and shortening. Add to dry ingredients and stir only enough to mix. Pour batter into a greased 8×8in baking pan. Bake at 425°F (hot oven) for 25 minutes. YIELD: 1 large loaf.

Special Spoonbread

Milk	3 cups
Cornmeal	1 cup
Salt	$1\frac{1}{2}$ teaspoons
Butter or margarine	2 tablespoons
Egg yolks, beaten	4
Egg whites	4

Combine milk, cornmeal and salt. Cook over low heat, stirring constantly, until thickened, about 15 minutes. Mix in fat. Cool to lukewarm. Stir in egg yolks. Beat egg whites until stiff, but not dry. Fold into mixture; pour into greased 1½ quart casserole. Bake at 400°F (hot oven) for 35 to 40 minutes or until set. YIELD: Serves 6.

Gingerbread

Sifted flour	1½ cups
Baking soda	¼ teaspoon
Baking powder	1 teaspoon
Sugar	¼ cup
Salt	¼ teaspoon
Ginger	1 teaspoon
Cinnamon	1 teaspoon
Ground cloves	¼ teaspoon
Milk	½ cup
Eggs, beaten	1
Molasses	½ cup
Melted shortening *or* oil	¼ cup

Sift together dry ingredients. Add milk to beaten egg. Pour into dry ingredients and stir until smooth. Stir in molasses and shortening. Pour batter into greased shallow pan, about 8in sq. Bake at 350°F (moderate oven) for 30 to 40 minutes. YIELD: 1 large loaf.

Spiced Prune Bread

Shortening	½ cup
Sugar	1 cup
Eggs, well beaten	2
Finely chopped, cooked prunes	1¼ cups
Sifted flour	2 cups
Baking soda	1½ teaspoons

Cinnamon	1 teaspoon
Cloves	¾ teaspoon
Salt	¾ teaspoon
Sour milk	½ cup

Cream shortening and add sugar. Cream until fluffy. Add eggs and beat well. Blend in prunes. Sift together flour, soda, spices and salt. Add to creamed mixture in three portions alternately with the sour milk in two portions. Turn into a greased shallow pan about 12 · 8in. Bake at 350°F (moderate oven) for 35 to 40 minutes. YIELD: 1 large loaf.

Vanilla Flavored Nut Bread

Sugar	⅔ cup
Shortening	¼ cup
Eggs	2
Sifted flour	2 cups
Baking powder	3 teaspoons
Salt	½ teaspoon
Orange juice *or* milk	1 cup
Vanilla	½ teaspoon
Chopped nuts	⅔ cup

Beat sugar, shortening and eggs until creamy. Mix flour, baking powder and salt thoroughly. Stir into egg mixture alternately with liquid and vanilla; stir nuts into last portion of flour mixture before blending it into batter. Pour into greased 9 × 5 × 3in loaf pan. Bake at 350°F (moderate oven) for 50 to 60 minutes, or until no batter clings to toothpick inserted in centre of loaf. Remove from pan and cool on rack. YIELD: 1 loaf.

Corn Rice Bread

Pre-cooked rice	⅔ cup
Water	¾ cup
Milk	¾ cup
Cornmeal	1 cup

Sifted all-purpose	
flour	$\frac{1}{2}$ cup
Baking powder	2 teaspoons
Salt	$\frac{1}{2}$ teaspoon
Butter	3 tablespoons
Sugar	$\frac{1}{4}$ cup
Eggs, beaten	1

Combine rice, water and milk; set aside. Sift together corn-meal, flour, baking powder and salt. Cream butter and sugar. Add egg and beat well. Stir in rice mixture. Add sifted dry in-gredients and beat slowly with a rotary beater until flour is moistened. Pour into a greased 8in sq pan. Bake at 400°F (hot oven) for 30 minutes, or until lightly browned. Serve hot with butter. YIELD: Serves 9.

Apple Sauce Nut Bread

Prepared biscuit	
mix*	2$\frac{1}{2}$ cups
Uncooked rolled	
oats	1 cup
Salt	$\frac{1}{2}$ teaspoon
Baking powder	2 teaspoons
Eggs	1
Honey	1 cup
Apple sauce	1 cup
Golden raisins	1 cup
Coarsely chopped	
walnuts	1 cup

Measure biscuit mix; combine with oats, salt and baking powder. Beat egg slightly; add honey and apple sauce. Beat quickly into biscuit mix. Stir in raisins and walnuts. Pour batter into 9 × 5 × 3in lined, greased loaf pan. Let stand 10 minutes before baking to keep fruit and nuts from sinking to the bottom. Bake at 350°F (moderate) for 60 to 70 minutes or until done in centre when tested. Cool in pan 10 minutes before removing to rack. YIELD: 1 loaf.

* See pp 19–20 for alternative to prepared biscuit mix.

Pineapple Brunch Bread

Crushed pineapple in syrup	1 can (13¼oz)
Biscuit mix*	2¼ cups
Honey	¼ cup
Melted butter *or* margarine	2 tablespoons
Eggs	1
Milk	¾ cup
Honey and Butter Topping:	
Soft butter *or* margarine	¼ cup
Honey	⅓ cup
Reserved crushed pineapple	½ cup

HONEY AND BUTTER TOPPING: Blend together soft butter or margarine, honey and reserved crushed pineapple (see below).

Drain crushed pineapple—save syrup for use in beverage or gelatine. Combine biscuit mix with honey, butter, egg and milk. Stir until thoroughly blended. Reserve ½ cup crushed pineapple for topping. Stir remaining fruit into batter. Pour into well greased 8 × 8 × 2in pan. Carefully spread honey and butter topping over batter. Heat oven to 400°F (hot). Bake 30 to 35 minutes or until done. Serve warm. YIELD: 1 loaf.

* See pp 19–20 for alternative to prepared biscuit mix.

Nutty Olive Loaf

Sifted all-purpose flour	3 cups
Baking powder	4 teaspoons
Salt	1 teaspoon
Soft butter *or* margarine	½ cup

Finely chopped pimento-stuffed olives	$\frac{2}{3}$ cup
Coarsely chopped walnuts	$\frac{1}{2}$ cup
Milk	$\frac{2}{3}$ cup
Eggs, well beaten	2
Mild flavored honey	$\frac{3}{4}$ cup

Sift flour, baking powder and salt into medium-size mixing bowl. Cut in butter with pastry blender or rub in with fingers, until mixture resembles coarse cornmeal. Fold in olives and nuts. Combine milk, eggs, and honey. Make a well in centre of flour mixture. Add egg mixture all at once. Stir to moisten dry ingredients (batter will not be smooth). Do not beat. Spoon into greased 9 × 5 × 3in loaf pan. Heat oven to 350°F (moderate). Bake 55 to 60 minutes. Cool in pan 10 minutes. Remove from pan and continue cooling on wire rack. Bread slices thinner if stored overnight or frozen. YIELD: 1 loaf.

SUGGESTION: Batter may be made into muffins. Grease bottoms of 18 ($2\frac{1}{2}$in) muffin pan cups. Heat oven to 400°F (hot). Bake 20 to 30 minutes or until done. Remove from pan. Serve piping hot.

Shortbread

Butter *or* margarine	$\frac{1}{2}$ cup
Brown sugar	$\frac{1}{3}$ cup, packed
Chopped or diced roasted almonds	$\frac{1}{2}$ cup
Sifted all-purpose flour	$1\frac{1}{4}$ cups

Cream butter and sugar together. Stir in almonds and flour. Shape into 2 large rounds about $\frac{1}{4}$in thick and $6\frac{1}{2}$in in diameter, mark off into pie-shaped wedges. Or roll dough $\frac{1}{4}$in thick on lightly floured board, and cut into individual wedges. Bake in

350°F (moderate oven) for 15 minutes or until edges are very lightly browned. YIELD: 2 shortbreads or about 4 dozen smaller wedges.

Banana Almond Bread

Brown sugar	¾ cup
Mashed banana	1 cup (3 bananas)
Eggs	1
Milk	½ cup
Biscuit mix*	3 cups
Diced, roasted almonds	1 cup

In a mixing bowl, beat together sugar, banana, egg, milk and biscuit mix. Stir in almonds. Turn into a greased 9 × 5 × 3in baking pan. Bake in 350°F (moderate) oven for 45 minutes or until done. Cool. YIELD: 18 to 20 slices.

* See pp 19–20 for alternative to prepared biscuit mix.

Pioneer Spoonbread

Condensed cream of chicken *or* mushroom soup	1 can (10½oz)
Milk	1 soup can
Cornmeal	½ cup
Butter *or* margarine	2 tablespoons
Eggs, separated	2

Stir soup until smooth; gradually blend in milk. Add cornmeal; cook until thickened, stirring. Add butter; remove from heat. Beat egg yolks until thick and lemon-colored; stir into mixture. Beat egg whites until stiff but not dry; fold into mixture. Pour into buttered 1 quart casserole. Bake in a 350°F (moderate) oven for 1 hour or until golden brown. Serve with butter or syrup. YIELD: 1 large loaf.

Peanut Butter Bread

Sifted flour	2 cups
Baking powder	3 teaspoons
Salt	1½ teaspoons
Sugar	⅓ cup
Orange rind	1 teaspoon
Peanut butter	1 cup
Eggs	2
Milk	1¼ cups

Mix and sift flour, baking powder, salt, sugar and orange rind. Cut in peanut butter with two knives or rub in with fingertips. Combine slightly beaten eggs and milk, add to dry ingredients and stir just enough to moisten. Pour the mixture into a 9 × 5 × 3in loaf pan. Bake at 350°F (moderate oven) for about 1 hour and 10 minutes. YIELD: 1 loaf.

Buttermilk Brown Bread

Whole wheat flour	2 cups
Buttermilk	1 cup
Molasses	½ cup
Sugar	2 tablespoons
Salt	¼ teaspoon
Baking soda	1 teaspoon
Hot water	2 tablespoons
Puffed, seeded muscat raisins	1¼ cups

Mix whole wheat flour with buttermilk, molasses, sugar, salt and baking soda mixed with hot water. Fold in raisins. Pour batter into a greased 9 × 5 × 3in bread pan lined with buttered waxed paper. Bake at 350°F (moderate oven) for about 50 minutes. Cool on rack. YIELD: 1 loaf.

Raisin Fruit Bread

Sifted all-purpose flour	1½ cups
Baking powder	1 teaspoon
Baking soda	1 teaspoon
Salt	½ teaspoon
Cinnamon	1 teaspoon
Nutmeg	1 teaspoon
Brown sugar	½ cup (firmly packed)
Seedless raisins	1 cup
Rolled oats, uncooked	1 cup
Eggs, beaten	2
Vegetable oil	⅓ cup
Apple sauce	1 cup

Mix and sift flour, baking powder, baking soda, salt and spices. Stir in sugar, raisins and oats. Add remaining ingredients; stir only until dry ingredients are moistened. Pour into greased 9 × 5 × 3in loaf pan. Bake at 350°F (moderate oven) for 1 hour. Remove from pan immediately. Cool. Wrap cooled bread and store one day for ease in slicing. YIELD: 1 large loaf.

Fruit Tasty Bread

Shortening	¼ cup
Sugar	⅔ cup
Eggs, well beaten	2
Sifted, all-purpose flour	2 cups
Baking powder	1 teaspoon
Baking soda	1 teaspoon
Salt	1 teaspoon
Coarsely grated raw apple	2 cups
Grated lemon peel	1 tablespoon
Chopped walnuts	⅔ cup

Cream shortening and sugar until light and fluffy; beat in eggs. Mix and sift flour, baking powder, baking soda and salt; add alternately with the grated apple to egg mixture. Stir in lemon peel and walnuts (batter will be stiff). Bake in greased and floured loaf pan, 9 × 5 × 3in, at 350°F (moderate oven) for 50 to 60 minutes. Do not slice until cold. YIELD: 1 large loaf.

Deluxe Corn Bread

Cornmeal	1¼ cups
Sifted all-purpose flour	¾ cup
Sugar	¼ cup
Baking powder	1 tablespoon
Salt	½ teaspoon
Eggs	1
Milk	1 cup
Vegetable oil	¼ cup

Sift together cornmeal, flour, sugar, baking powder and salt into bowl. Add egg, milk and oil. Beat with rotary beater until smooth, about 1 minute. Bake in greased 8in sq baking pan in preheated hot oven, 425°F, for 20 to 25 minutes. YIELD: serves 9.

VARIATIONS: *Parsley and Celery Seed:* Add 1 tablespoon chopped parsley and ½ teaspoon celery seed to batter.

Corn: Add 1 cup drained whole kernel to batter.

Whole Wheat Yeast Bread

Warm water	2 cups
Sugar	1 teaspoon
Active dry yeast *or*	2 packages
Compressed yeast	2 cakes
Whole wheat flour	5½–6 cups
Salt	1 tablespoon
Brown sugar	1 tablespoon
Shortening (lard)	1 tablespoon

In a bowl dissolve 1 teaspoon of sugar in the warm water and sprinkle on dried yeast or crumble in fresh yeast. Leave until frothy, about 10 minutes. In a large bowl mix whole wheat flour, salt, brown sugar and cut or rub in shortening. Add the yeast liquid and mix to a soft dough. Turn out on to lightly floured board; knead until smooth and elastic, about 8 to 10 minutes. Place in greased bowl, turning to grease top. Cover with polythene sheet, let rise in warm place until doubled in bulk, about one hour. Punch dough down and divide into two. Shape each piece of dough into a round cob, approx 6in in diameter, place on a floured baking sheet. Mark a cross on the top with a sharp knife. Cover and let rise in warm place until doubled in bulk, about 1 hour. Bake at 450°F (hot oven) for 25 to 30 minutes or until done. Remove from baking sheet and cool on wire rack. YIELD: 2 loaves.

Irish Soda Bread

Whole wheat flour	2 cups less 2 tablespoons
Sifted all-purpose flour	2 cups
Salt	1 teaspoon
Baking soda	2 teaspoons
Shortening	2 tablespoons
Buttermilk	1½ cups

Put the whole wheat flour into a large bowl. Sift the all-purpose flour, salt and baking soda on to it and stir to mix. Cut or rub in the shortening. Pour in the buttermilk and mix well to form a soft dough (a little more milk may be added, if necessary). Turn dough out on to a board floured with whole wheat flour and knead lightly until smooth. Form into a round and place on a greased baking sheet or in a greased 7in round pan. Sprinkle a little whole wheat flour on top. Cut a deep cross with a sharp knife. Bake in preheated oven 425°F (hot) for 10 minutes, then reduce heat to 400°F and bake for a further 30 minutes. Cool on a wire rack. YIELD: 1 large loaf.

3

Rolls

Fragrant, crusty, home-baked rolls may be enjoyed with a main dish, or as treats by themselves. Just break open a fresh roll, spread with butter or fruit jams, and enter a world of good, old-fashioned taste. Rolls can be simple or festive and offer good eating for everyone.

Apricot Twist Rolls

Hot roll mix*	1 package (13¾oz)
Dairy sour cream	½ cup
Apricot jam	½ cup
Shredded coconut	1 cup
Apricot jam	2 tablespoons

Prepare dough according to package* directions. Cover and allow to stand in warm place until doubled (about 30 minutes). Divide in half. On lightly floured surface roll half to measure 8 × 12in. Spread with ¼ cup sour cream, ¼ cup apricot jam and sprinkle with ½ cup coconut. From long side of rectangle, fold over by thirds. Cut into 12 strips. With a wide spatula, carefully lift and twist each strip as placed on large buttered baking sheet. Repeat with second half of dough. Bake in preheated 375°F (moderate) oven for 20 to 25 minutes. TIP: To glaze, brush with 2 tablespoons warmed apricot jam immediately after removal from oven. YIELD: 24 rolls.

* See pp 20–21 for alternative to hot roll mix.

Almond Beehive Rolls

Brown sugar	1 cup (packed)
Butter *or* margarine	½ cup
Water	⅓ cup
Cinnamon	½ teaspoon
Almonds, toasted and slivered	⅔ cup
Baking powder biscuit mix (home-made *or* package)	4 cups

Combine brown sugar, butter, water and cinnamon and heat slowly, stirring occasionally, until butter is melted. Add almonds and spoon into greased custard cups or muffin pans. Prepare biscuit dough according to directions to about ¾in thick; cut with 2in round cutter. Place a biscuit in each cup. Bake in 400°F (hot) oven for 12 to 14 minutes or until biscuits are baked. Let stand 3 or 4 minutes, then invert to remove. Serve warm. YIELD: About 20 rolls.

* See pp 19–20 for alternative to baking powder biscuit mix.

Sweet Glazed Rolls

Chopped nuts	¼ cup
Fruit sauce (apple, cranberry, pear, etc)	½ cup
Brown sugar	¼ cup (packed)
Brown 'n' serve rolls	6 to 8

Pre-set oven at 400°F (hot). Grease 6 or 8 muffin pans or custard cups. Sprinkle a few chopped nuts into each. Combine fruit sauce, crushed with a fork, and brown sugar. Put a tablespoon of the mixture in each muffin cup. Then turn brown'n'-serve rolls upside down and press into each muffin cup. Bake at 400°F (hot oven) for 12 to 15 minutes. Let cool for 4 to 5 minutes. Invert pans and gently remove rolls. YIELD: 6 to 8 rolls.

Morning Rolls

Warm milk	¾ cup
Warm water	½ cup
Sugar	1 teaspoon
Active dry yeast *or*	1 package
Compressed yeast	1 cake
Sifted all-purpose flour	4 cups
Salt	1 teaspoon
Shortening	¼ cup

Place warm milk and water in a bowl and stir in sugar. Sprinkle on dried yeast and allow to stand until frothy, about 10 minutes, *or* crumble in compressed yeast and stir until dissolved. Place flour and salt in a large mixing bowl and cut or rub in shortening. Add yeast liquid and mix to form a firm dough, adding a little extra flour if needed. Turn out on to a lightly floured board and knead for 5 minutes. Cover and let rise until doubled in size, about 1 hour in a warm place. Punch down and divide into 12 equal pieces. Shape each into a ball and roll out to an oval about ½in thick. Place on floured baking sheet and dredge tops with flour. Cover; let rise until double in size, about 30 to 40 minutes, in a warm place. Press each roll gently in the centre with three fingers to prevent blisters. Bake at 400°F (hot oven) for 15 to 20 minutes. Cool on a wire rack. YIELD: 12 rolls.

Barbecue Buns

Unsifted flour	5¾–6¾ cups
Instant non-fat dry milk solids	⅓ cup

Sugar	$\frac{1}{4}$ cup
Salt	1 tablespoon
Active dry yeast *or*	2 packages
Compressed yeast	2 cakes
Margarine, softened	$\frac{1}{3}$ cup
Warm water	2 cups

In large bowl, thoroughly mix 2 cups flour, dry milk solids, sugar, salt and *undissolved* yeast. Add margarine. Gradually add warm water to dry ingredients and beat 2 minutes at medium speed of electric mixer, scraping bowl occasionally. Add $\frac{3}{4}$ cup flour. Beat at high speed 2 minutes, scraping bowl occasionally. Stir in enough additional flour to make a stiff dough. Turn out on to lightly floured board; knead until smooth and elastic, about 8 to 10 minutes. Place in a greased bowl, turning to grease top. Cover with plastic or polythene sheet; let rise in warm place, free from draught, until doubled in bulk, about 45 minutes. Punch dough down; let rise again until nearly doubled, about 20 minutes. Divide dough in half; cut each half into 10 equal pieces. Form each piece into a smooth round ball. Place on greased baking sheets about 2in apart; press to flatten. Cover with oiled plastic or polythene sheet; let rise in warm place, free from draught, until doubled in bulk, about 1 hour. Bake at 375°F (moderate oven) for 15 to 20 minutes or until done. Remove from baking sheets and cool on wire racks. YIELD: 20 buns.

VARIATIONS: *Chive Barbecue Buns:* Prepare as recipe directs but add $\frac{1}{4}$ cup (4 tablespoons) chopped chives to dry ingredients. Brush while warm with melted margarine.

Sesame Seed Barbecue Buns: Prepare as recipe directs but add $\frac{1}{4}$ cup (4 tablespoons) toasted sesame seeds to dry ingredients. Before baking, brush buns with combined egg white and 2 tablespoons water and sprinkle with additional sesame seeds.

Dill Barbecue Buns: Prepare as recipe directs but add 2 tablespoons dill seed to dry ingredients. Brush while warm with melted margarine.

Celery Seed Barbecue Buns: Prepare as recipe directs but add 2½ teaspoons celery seeds to dry ingredients. Brush while warm with melted margarine.

Dinner Rolls à la Parmesan

Active dry yeast	1 package
Warm water (105–115°F)	⅔ cup
All-purpose buttermilk biscuit mix*	2½ cups
Soft butter *or* margarine	1 tablespoon
Grated Parmesan cheese	2 tablespoons
Garlic powder	1 teaspoon

Dissolve yeast in warm water. Stir in baking mix;* beat vigorously. Turn dough on to floured board. Knead until smooth, about 20 times. Roll dough into a rectangle, 12 × 9in. Spread with butter; sprinkle with cheese and garlic powder. Roll up from long side. Cut into 12 rolls. Cover with oiled polythene sheet and let rise in a warm place until double in size, about 30 minutes. Heat oven to 400°F (hot oven). Bake 10 to 15 minutes or until golden brown. YIELD: 1 dozen.

* See p 20 for alternative to all-purpose buttermilk biscuit mix.

Orange Rolls

All-purpose buttermilk biscuit mix*	2⅓ cups
Sugar	2 tablespoons
Butter *or* margarine, melted	3 tablespoons
Milk	½ cup
Soft butter *or* margarine	2 tablespoons
Orange marmalade	½ cup

Preheat oven to 425°F (hot oven). Meanwhile, stir baking mix, sugar, 3 tablespoons butter or margarine and the milk to a soft dough. Gently smooth dough into a ball on floured board. Knead 8 to 10 times. Roll dough into a rectangle, 15 × 19in. Spread with 2 tablespoons butter or margarine and the marmalade. Roll up, beginning at wide side. Seal well by pinching edge of dough into roll. Cut into 1in slices. Bake on greased baking sheet in hot oven for 12 to 15 minutes. Serve warm. YIELD: 15 rolls.

* See p 20 for alternative to all-purpose buttermilk biscuit mix.

4

Muffins

Oven-warmed muffins give a lift to the appetite and the menu when offered by themselves or as part of a meal. Delicious muffins can be enjoyed with almost any other food item, or by themselves with a butter or jam pat. You will discover a marvellous culinary taste thrill when making a muffin sandwich. Good eating is improved by the appearance of aromatic home-baked muffins on the table before you.

Home-Spun Muffins

Sifted all-purpose flour	2 cups
Sugar	2–4 tablespoons
Baking powder	$2\frac{1}{2}$ teaspoons
Salt	$\frac{1}{2}$ teaspoon
Eggs, well beaten	1
Milk	1 cup
Melted shortening or cooking oil	2–4 tablespoons

Sift dry ingredients together into a mixing bowl. Combine the beaten egg, milk and cooled melted shortening or oil. Make a well in the dry ingredients. Add the liquid mixture and stir just enough to combine. The mixture should have a rough appearance. Fill greased muffin pans $\frac{2}{3}$ full. Bake at 425°F (hot oven) until golden brown (about 20 to 30 minutes). No changes are required for preparation at altitudes up to 10,000ft. YIELD: 12 muffins.

VARIATIONS: *Blueberry Muffins:* Use ¼ cup sugar and ¼ cup shortening. Add ¾–1 cup of frozen or well-drained, canned blueberries to the batter and stir in carefully.

Cheese Muffins: Add 1 cup grated Cheddar cheese and ¼ cup milk.

Date Nut Muffins: Add ½ cup chopped dates, ½ cup chopped nuts and 1 tablespoon milk.

Whole Wheat Muffins: Substitute ⅔ cup whole wheat flour for ⅔ cup all-purpose flour.

Ginger Muffins

Sugar	⅔ cup
Dark molasses	⅔ cup
Melted shortening *or* oil	⅓ cup
Eggs, beaten	1
Sifted flour	2 cups
Cinnamon	1½ teaspoons
Nutmeg	¼ teaspoon
Ginger	1½ teaspoons
Baking soda	1½ teaspoons
Buttermilk	⅔ cup

Mix sugar, molasses and shortening with the egg. Sift together the flour, cinnamon, nutmeg, ginger and baking soda. Add dry ingredients alternately with the buttermilk to the egg mixture, stirring just enough to blend. Pour the batter into greased muffin pans. Bake at 425°F (hot oven) for about 15 minutes. YIELD: 12 medium-sized muffins.

Popovers

Eggs	3
Milk	1 cup
Melted fat *or* oil	2 tablespoons
Flour	1 cup
Salt	½ teaspoon

Grease muffin pans and place them in an oven that is pre-heating at 450°F (very hot). Next—beat eggs well in a large mixing bowl. Add milk and fat. Mix flour and salt; add to liquid mixture. Beat until smooth. Fill hot muffin pans half full of batter. Bake at 450°F (very hot oven) for 15 minutes; reduce heat to 375°F (moderate oven) and bake 10 minutes longer. Do not open oven door during baking. Immediately after baking, insert a paring knife through the top of each popover to allow steam to escape. YIELD: 12 popovers.

Muffins Magnifique

Eggs	1
Milk	1 cup
Melted shortening *or* oil	$\frac{1}{3}$ cup
Flour	2 cups
Baking powder	1 tablespoon
Salt	1 teaspoon
Sugar	$\frac{1}{3}$ cup

Beat egg until yolk and white are well blended. Blend in milk and shortening. Mix dry ingredients thoroughly. Add liquid and stir until dry ingredients are barely moistened. Do not overmix. Batter should be lumpy. Fill greased muffin pans half full of batter. Bake at 400°F (hot oven) for 20 to 25 minutes. YIELD: 12 muffins.

VARIATIONS: *Blueberry Muffins:* Increase sugar to $\frac{1}{2}$ cup. Lightly blend in $\frac{3}{4}$ cup fresh or drained canned blueberries when combining liquid and dry ingredients. Do not crush berries.

Bran Muffins: Reduce flour to $1\frac{1}{4}$ cups. Mix 2 cups bran flakes or raisin bran cereal with dry ingredients before adding liquid.

Oatmeal Raisin Muffins: Reduce flour to $1\frac{1}{4}$ cups. Mix 1 cup quick-cooking rolled oats and $\frac{1}{2}$ cup raisins with dry ingredients before adding liquid.

Farmer Boy Corn Muffins

Sifted all-purpose flour	1 cup
Yellow cornmeal	1 cup
Baking powder	3 teaspoons
Sugar	$\frac{1}{4}$ cup
Salt	1 teaspoon
Eggs, well beaten	1
Milk	1 cup
Melted *or* liquid shortening	$\frac{1}{4}$ cup

Sift together dry ingredients; combine egg, milk and shortening. Add liquids to flour mixture, stirring only until ingredients are wet. Do not try to beat out the lumps. Spoon into well-greased muffin pans. Bake at 400°F (hot oven) for about 20 minutes or until done. YIELD: 12 muffins.

Orange Muffins

Coarsely grated orange rind	$\frac{1}{2}$ cup (rind of 2 large oranges)
Sugar	$\frac{1}{2}$ cup + $\frac{1}{4}$ cup
Water	$\frac{1}{4}$ cup
Salad oil	$\frac{1}{4}$ cup
Orange juice	$\frac{3}{4}$ cup
Eggs, beaten	1
Sifted all-purpose flour	2 cups
Baking powder	$2\frac{1}{2}$ teaspoons
Salt	$\frac{1}{2}$ teaspoon
Baking soda	$\frac{1}{4}$ teaspoon
Finely chopped pecans, optional	$\frac{1}{2}$ cup

Combine orange rind, $\frac{1}{2}$ cup sugar and water in small saucepan. Cook slowly for 5 minutes, stirring constantly. Remove from heat. Cool. Add salad oil, orange juice and egg. Sift together flour, baking powder, salt, baking soda and remaining ¼ cup sugar. Add orange mixture all at once to flour mixture; add pecans. Stir only until dry ingredients are dampened. Turn into greased muffin cups, filling each about ⅔ full. Bake at 400°F (hot oven) for 20 to 25 minutes or until done. Serve warm. YIELD: 18 muffins.

Dinner Muffins

Eggs	1
Milk	1 cup
Salad Oil	¼ cup
All-purpose sifted flour	2 cups
Sugar	¼ cup
Baking powder	3 teaspoons
Salt	1 teaspoon

Heat oven to 400°F (hot oven). Grease bottoms of 12 medium muffin cups. Beat eggs stir in milk and oil. Mix in remaining ingredients just until flour is moistened. Batter should be lumpy. Fill prepared muffin cups ⅔ full. Bake 20 to 25 minutes in hot oven or until golden brown. Immediately remove from pan. YIELD: 12 muffins.

VARIATIONS: *Cheese Muffins:* Add 1 cup shredded Cheddar cheese with the flour.

Tangy Muffins: Add ½ cup chopped pimento-stuffed olives and ½ cup coarsely chopped walnuts with the flour.

Herb Muffins: Add 1 teaspoon dill seed and 1 teaspoon instant minced onion or 1 tablespoon finely chopped fresh onion with the oil.

Dinner Popovers

Eggs	4
Milk	2 cups
Sifted all-purpose flour	2 cups
Salt	1 teaspoon

Heat oven to 450°F (very hot oven). Grease 12 deep custard cups or 16 medium muffin cups. With rotary beater, beat eggs slightly. Add milk, flour and salt; beat just until smooth. *Do not overbeat.* Fill prepared custard cups ½ full, muffin cups ¾ full. Bake 25 minutes. Lower oven temperature to 350°F (moderate oven) and bake 15 to 20 minutes longer or until golden brown. Remove immediately and serve hot. YIELD: Makes 12 to 16.

Honey Butter Cinnamon Buns

Warm water	⅔ cup
Active dry yeast *or*	1 package
Compressed yeast cake	1 package
Honey	½ cup
Eggs	1
Salt	½ teaspoon
Dry milk powder	2 tablespoons
Mixed candied fruit *or* raisins, chopped	¼ cup
Chopped pecans	¼ cup
Sifted all-purpose flour	2 cups
Cinnamon, optional	½ teaspoon

Measure warm water into large mixing bowl. Sprinkle or crumble yeast over water; stir until dissolved. Combine honey, egg, salt and dry milk. Add to yeast mixture; blend well. Add fruit, nuts and flour. Stir to mix; then beat until batter is shiny and smooth, about 2 minutes. Scrape sides of bowl. Cover with a plastic or polythene sheet and let rise in a warm place, free from draught, to double in size, about 45 minutes. Stir down and drop by spoonfuls into 12 greased muffin pans. Let rise in warm place, covered, free from draught, until doubled, about 30 minutes. Bake at 350°F (moderate oven) for 20 to 25 minutes. Remove from pan; serve warm. YIELD: 12 buns.

Cherry Pink Muffins

Sifted all-purpose flour	1¾ cups
Salt	½ teaspoon
Baking powder	2½ teaspoons
Maraschino cherries, finely cut	½ cup
Eggs	1
Milk	¼ cup
Maraschino cherry juice	¼ cup
Salad oil	⅓ cup
Mild flavored honey	⅓ cup

Sift together dry ingredients. Drain cherries, reserving juice. Finely cut and measure ½ cup cherries. Beat egg slightly. Add milk, cherry juice, salad oil, honey and cherries. Make a well in centre of flour mixture. Pour in egg mixture all at once. Stir quickly, just until dry ingredients are moistened. Do not beat. (Batter will be lumpy.) Quickly spoon batter into 12 (2½in) greased muffin pan cups. Heat oven to 400°F (hot oven). Bake 12 to 15 minutes or until done. Serve piping hot. YIELD: 12 muffins.

Almond Orange Muffins

Almonds, blanched and sliced	½ cup
Butter or margarine	2 tablespoons
Brown sugar	¼ cup, packed
Orange muffin mix*	½ package (14oz)
Orange juice	¼ cup

Lightly toast almonds. Cream butter and sugar; gently stir in almonds. Spoon into 6 to 8 well-greased muffin cups. Prepare muffin mix as package directs, substituting orange juice for water. Divide evenly into muffin cups. Bake as package directs or at 400°F (hot oven) for 20 to 25 minutes. Remove from oven and turn out immediately. Serve warm. YIELD: 6 to 8 muffins.

VARIATION: Using the same almond mixture as topping, prepare a blueberry muffin mix package according to directions, in place of the orange muffin mix.

* See p 20 for alternative to orange muffin mix or use half the quantity of the recipe for Orange Muffins on p 43, omitting the pecans.

Skim Milk Popovers

Flour	$\frac{3}{4}$ cup
Salt	$\frac{1}{4}$ teaspoon
Medium eggs	2
Skim milk	$\frac{3}{4}$ cup
Melted butter	$\frac{1}{2}$ teaspoon
Soft butter	$1\frac{1}{4}$ teaspoons

Mix flour and salt. Beat eggs; add milk and $\frac{1}{2}$ teaspoon melted butter. Add liquid mixture to dry ingredients and beat for 2 minutes. Using $1\frac{1}{4}$ teaspoons soft butter, grease 8 muffin cups. Fill $\frac{2}{3}$ with batter. Bake at 400°F (hot oven) for 40 minutes. Remove from oven and serve promptly. YIELD: 8 popovers.

Peanut Butter Muffins

Sifted flour	2 cups
Baking powder	1 tablespoon
Salt	$\frac{3}{4}$ teaspoon
Seedless raisins	$\frac{1}{2}$ cup
Butter	2 tablespoons
Chunk-style peanut butter	$\frac{1}{2}$ cup
Dark brown sugar	$\frac{1}{3}$ cup
Eggs, well beaten	1
Milk	$1\frac{1}{2}$ cups

Mix and sift flour, baking powder and salt. Stir in raisins. Next, cream butter and peanut butter together; add sugar gradually and cream thoroughly. Combine egg and milk; add to creamed mixture alternately with sifted dry ingredients. Do not overbeat, just moisten dry ingredients. Fill buttered muffin cups about ⅔ full. Bake at 400°F (hot oven) for 30 to 35 minutes. YIELD: 15 medium muffins.

Sesame Raised Corn Meal Muffins

Compressed yeast *or*	1 cake
Active dry yeast	1 package
Warm water	¼ cup
Milk, scalded	2 cups
Cornmeal	1 cup
Sugar	½ cup
Salt	1 tablespoon
Butter *or* margarine	½ cup
Sifted all-purpose flour	4 cups
Eggs	2
Sesame seeds	For sprinkling tops

Dissolve yeast in lukewarm water. Pour scalded milk over cornmeal, sugar, salt and butter. Stir occasionally until butter melts; cool to lukewarm. Beat in 1 cup flour and eggs. Add dissolved or reconstituted yeast. Beat in remaining flour. (Batter will be very stiff.) Cover and let rise in warm place until double in size, about 1 hour. Stir batter down with wooden spoon. Fill greased, medium-sized muffin cups ¾ full. Cover; let rise in warm place until nearly double in size, about 45 minutes. Sprinkle with sesame seeds. Bake in preheated hot oven 400°F for about 15 minutes or until golden brown. Serve hot. YIELD: 2 dozen.

Holiday Muffins

Orange muffin mix*	1 package (14oz)
Finely chopped nuts	1 cup
Canned whole cranberry sauce, drained	¾ cup

For fancy slices at tea parties, collect 6 (6oz) empty frozen juice concentrate cans. Wash, dry and grease sides and bottoms thoroughly. Preheat oven to 375°F (moderate). Prepare muffin mix (using both envelopes) according to directions on package or make up muffin mix and use 14oz of it. Fold in whole cranberry sauce and nuts. Spoon batter into greased cans, filling ⅔ full. Bake at 375°F (moderate oven) for 30 to 35 minutes. Cool on rack 5 minutes. Ease out of cans with spatula. Cool. Slice to serve. For very thin slices, cool thoroughly, wrap in aluminium foil. Wait until second day to slice, or freeze wrapped rolls to keep for later use. YIELD: 6 very large triple-sized muffins to be sliced to individual servings.

* See p 20 for alternative to orange muffin mix.

Holiday Berry Muffins

Fresh cranberries, halved	¾ cup
Powdered sugar	½ cup
Flour	2 cups
Baking powder	3 teaspoons
Salt	½ teaspoon
Sugar	¼ cup
Eggs, well beaten	1
Milk	1 cup
Shortening, melted	4 tablespoons

Mix cranberry halves with powdered sugar and let stand while preparing muffin mixture. Sift dry ingredients. Add milk, egg and melted shortening all at once; mix until dry ingredients are dampened; do not beat. Fold in sugared cranberries. Fill muffin pans ⅔ full. Bake at 350°F (moderate oven) for 20 minutes. YIELD: 1 dozen.

Spicy Holiday Fruit Muffins

Fruit sauce, any flavor	1 cup
Brown sugar	$\frac{1}{4}$ cup, packed
Flour	1 tablespoon
Chopped pecans	$\frac{1}{2}$ cup
Packaged biscuit mix*	1 cup
Sugar	3 tablespoons
Cinnamon	1 teaspoon
Nutmeg	$\frac{1}{4}$ teaspoon
Eggs	1
Milk	$\frac{3}{4}$ cup

TOPPING: Combine fruit sauce, sugar, flour and pecans. Spoon 1 tablespoon of mixture into each of 12 greased muffin pan cups.

MUFFIN: Stir together biscuit mix, sugar, cinnamon and nutmeg. Stir together egg and milk. Add to dry ingredients stirring just to moisten. Fill muffin cups $\frac{2}{3}$ full. Bake at 400°F (hot oven) for 15 minutes. Remove from oven and invert pan immediately.
YIELD: 1 dozen.

* See pp 19–20 for alternative to packaged biscuit mix.

5

Biscuits

Light, fluffy and fragrant biscuits are a treasure of good eating for everyone. Piping hot biscuits start the taste buds a-runnin' and the appetite a-soarin'. When embellished with warm butter or fresh fruit jam, the biscuits become a taste treat that make them the star attractions in the world of bread baking. Biscuits are easy to make and doubly easy to enjoy!

Home-Spun Biscuits

Sifted all-purpose flour	2 cups
Baking powder	2½ teaspoons
Salt	½ teaspoon
Shortening	¼ cup
Milk	¾ cup approx

Sift the dry ingredients into mixing bowl. Cut or rub the shortening into dry ingredients until the mixture looks like coarse cornmeal. Make a well in the centre. Add milk and stir quickly and lightly until well blended. The mixture should be soft but not sticky. Turn on to a lightly floured board or pastry cloth. Knead lightly, about 10 to 15 strokes. Pat or roll out to desired thickness. Cut with floured 2in round biscuit cutter and place on ungreased baking sheet. Bake at 450°F (hot oven) for 12 to 15 minutes or until golden brown. YIELD: About 16 biscuits, cut ½in thick and 2in in diameter. No changes are required for preparation at altitudes up to 10,000ft.

VARIATIONS: *Cheese Biscuits:* Add ½ cup grated Cheddar cheese to the sifted dry ingredients.

51

Orange Biscuits: Add 1½ teaspoons grated orange rind and substitute orange juice for the liquid.

Whole Wheat Biscuits: Substitute ½ cup whole wheat flour for ½ cup of all-purpose flour.

Herb Biscuits: Add ¼ teaspoon dry mustard, ½ teaspoon dry sage and 1¼ teaspoons caraway seeds to flour mixture.

Drop Biscuits: Increase milk to 1 cup. Drop from spoon on to greased baking sheet and bake as per above directions.

Orange Tea Biscuits: Add grated rind of 1 orange to dry ingredients. Before baking, press ½ cube of lump sugar, dipped in orange juice, into top of each biscuit.

Rich Fruit Biscuits

Sifted all-purpose flour	2 cups
Baking powder	3 teaspoons
Salt	½ teaspoon
Sugar	2 tablespoons
Butter	¼ cup
Dried fruit, currants *or* raisins	⅓ cup
Eggs, beaten	1
Milk	2 tablespoons

Into a mixing bowl sift together flour, baking powder, salt and sugar. Cut or rub in butter until mixture resembles coarse meal. Add and stir in dried fruit. Add beaten egg and milk and mix to form a fairly soft dough. Turn out on to a lightly floured board and knead very lightly until smooth. Pat or roll out to about ½in thick. Cut out biscuits with floured 2in diameter biscuit cutter. Place on greased and floured baking sheet. Brush tops with a little milk. Bake in preheated oven, 450°F (hot) for 8 to 10 minutes or until golden brown and well risen. Cool on a wire rack. YIELD: 10 to 12 biscuits.

Buttermilk Biscuits

Sifted all-purpose flour	2 cups
Baking powder	1 tablespoon
Salt	½ teaspoon
Baking soda	¼ teaspoon
Butter	6 tablespoons
Buttermilk	1 cup

Into a mixing bowl sift together flour, baking powder, salt and baking soda. Using pastry blender or 2 knives, cut in butter until mixture resembles coarse meal. Add buttermilk all at once; stir until dough clings together. On lightly floured surface knead lightly. Pat or roll about ½in thick. Cut out biscuits with floured 2in diameter biscuit cutter. Place on baking sheet; brush tops with a little buttermilk. Bake in preheated oven 450°F (hot) for 15 to 18 minutes. YIELD: 12 biscuits.

VARIATION: *Cheese Biscuits:* Sprinkle tops of biscuits with 1 cup shredded Cheddar cheese after brushing with buttermilk. Bake as above.

Biscuit Bubble Ring

Light brown sugar	¾ cup, packed
Cinnamon	1 teaspoon
Butter, melted	½ cup (1 stick)
Refrigerated biscuits	2 packages (8oz each)

In a small bowl, blend together sugar and cinnamon. Pour 2 tablespoons melted butter in bottom of large ring mold; sprinkle in 4 tablespoons of sugar-cinnamon mixture. Dip each biscuit in remaining melted butter; then roll in sugar-cinnamon mixture. Place 10 biscuits in bottom of mold overlapping edges slightly. Repeat with second layer. (NOTE: Use buttered ring mold, 6½ cup size.) Bake 12 to 15 minutes in preheated oven 400°F (hot). Allow to cool on wire rack about 5 minutes. Invert on to serving plate. YIELD: Serves 6 to 8.

Zesty Buttermilk Biscuits

Flour	$2\frac{2}{3}$ cups
Salt	1 teaspoon
Baking powder	$2\frac{1}{2}$ teaspoons
Baking soda	$\frac{1}{2}$ teaspoon
Butter	$\frac{1}{2}$ cup
Buttermilk	1 cup

Mix and sift flour, salt, baking powder and soda. Cut or rub in butter. Add buttermilk and mix just enough to moisten. Turn dough on to floured board; roll out to about $\frac{1}{2}$in thickness. Cut with floured biscuit cutter. Place on lightly greased baking sheet. Brush tops with milk. Bake at 450°F (very hot oven) for about 10 to 12 minutes. YIELD: 16 medium biscuits.

Easy Cream Biscuits

Sifted flour	$\frac{3}{4}$ cup
Baking powder	$1\frac{1}{4}$ teaspoons
Salt	$\frac{1}{2}$ teaspoon
Heavy cream	$\frac{1}{2}$ cup

Mix and sift flour, baking powder and salt. Make a well in centre of dry ingredients. Add cream all at once. Stir quickly and vigorously until ingredients are just moistened. With lightly floured hands, pat in rectangle $\frac{1}{2}$in thick on ungreased baking sheet. Cut with floured knife into 6 squares (do not separate). Brush tops with melted butter. Bake at 450°F (very hot oven) for 12 to 15 minutes, or until golden brown. YIELD: 6 biscuits.

VARIATION: *Herbed Biscuits:* Mix $\frac{1}{8}$ teaspoon thyme into dry ingredients before sifting.

Boston Tea Drops

Creamed cottage	
cheese	1 cup
Milk	6 tablespoons
Thyme	$\frac{1}{8}$ teaspoon
Biscuit mix*	2 cups

Beat cheese with egg beater until almost smooth. Add with milk and thyme to biscuit mix. Stir well with fork until blended. Dough will be sticky. Drop by spoonfuls on a well-greased baking sheet. Bake at 425°F (hot oven) for 10 to 15 minutes. Serve the moment they come from the oven. YIELD: 20 'drops' or biscuits.

* See pp 19–20 for alternative to packaged biscuit mix.

Fruit Flavored Tea Biscuits

Sifted all-purpose	
flour	2 cups
Baking powder	3 teaspoons
Baking soda	$\frac{1}{4}$ teaspoon
Salt	1 teaspoon
Shortening	3 tablespoons
Eggs	1
Fruit sauce, any	
flavor	1 cup
Sour cream	$\frac{1}{4}$ cup
Cheese, grated for	
sprinkling tops	

Sift dry ingredients together, and cut or rub in shortening. Beat egg until creamy, add fruit sauce and sour cream, and add to first mixture. Mix until dough clings together. Roll out on floured board and cut into square biscuits. Place on baking sheet and sprinkle with grated cheese. Bake at 400°F (moderate oven) for 15 to 20 minutes. YIELD: 1 dozen.

Fruity Griddle Biscuits

Sifted self-rising flour	2 cups
Salt	pinch
Nutmeg, grated	½ teaspoon
Shortening	¼ cup
Sugar	¼ cup
Dried fruit, currants, seedless raisins *or* sultanas	⅓ cup
Eggs, beaten	1
Milk	2 tablespoons

Into a mixing bowl sift together flour, salt and nutmeg. Cut or rub in shortening until mixture resembles coarse meal. Stir in sugar and dried fruit. Mix with egg and milk to form a stiff dough. Turn out on to a lightly floured board and roll out to about ½in thick and cut into 2in rounds or triangles. Heat a griddle to moderately hot and cook biscuits till brown on both sides, about 5 minutes on each side. Serve hot, split and buttered. YIELD: 10.

Whole Wheat Biscuits

Whole wheat flour	2 cups less 2 tablespoons
Salt	¼ teaspoon
Baking powder	2 teaspoons
Butter *or* margarine	2 tablespoons
Sugar	¼ cup
Eggs, beaten	1
Milk	4–6 tablespoons

Mix flour, salt and baking powder in a mixing bowl. Cut or rub in butter or margarine. Stir in the sugar. Mix to a fairly soft dough with beaten egg and milk. Turn out on to a lightly floured board and roll out ¾in thick and cut out into 10 to 12 rounds using a 2in cutter. Put on greased and floured baking sheet and bake in preheated hot oven, 450°F, for about 10 minutes. Cool on a wire rack. Split and serve buttered. YIELD: 10 to 12.

6

Waffles

Just inhale the spiralling goodness of morning waffles being made in the kitchen, and you'll be awake almost immediately. Nothing can compare with the early morning fragrance of freshly made waffles, waiting to be drenched in syrup or butter, eager to be enjoyed by the lucky diner. Yes, a waffle is worthy of being enjoyed with respect as a culinary art . . . for that is what a waffle should be—a culinary creation.

Waffles

Sifted flour	1½ cups
Baking powder	1½ teaspoons
Salt	½ teaspoon
Sugar	1 tablespoon
Eggs, separated	2
Milk	1 cup
Melted shortening *or*	
oil	2 tablespoons

Sift dry ingredients together. Beat egg yolks and whites separately. Combine egg yolks, milk and shortening. Mix with dry ingredients, stirring only until batter is smooth. Fold in beaten egg whites. Bake in a hot waffle baker. YIELD: 4 waffles.

Better Buttermilk Waffles

Sifted all-purpose flour	1½ cups
Sugar	1 tablespoon

Baking powder	1 teaspoon
Baking soda	$\frac{1}{2}$ teaspoon
Salt	$\frac{1}{2}$ teaspoon
Egg yolks, lightly beaten	2
Buttermilk	$1\frac{1}{2}$ cups
Butter, melted	6 tablespoons ($\frac{3}{4}$ stick)
Egg whites	2

Into a bowl, sift together flour, sugar, baking powder, baking soda and salt. Combine egg yolks, buttermilk and butter; stir into dry ingredients until smooth. Beat egg whites until stiff but not dry; carefully fold into batter. Bake in preheated waffle baker until golden brown. YIELD: 3 large waffles.

Rice Pancakes or Waffles

Pre-cooked rice	$\frac{2}{3}$ cup
Water	$\frac{2}{3}$ cup
Milk	$\frac{3}{4}$ cup
Egg yolks, lightly beaten	2
Liquid shortening (oil)	1 tablespoon
Pancake mix*	1 cup
Egg whites, stiffly beaten	2
Butter to serve	
Maple syrup to serve	

Combine rice and water; set aside. Mix milk, egg yolks and shortening in a bowl. Add pancake mixture and stir lightly until moistened. Stir in rice mixture. Fold in egg whites. Bake on a hot griddle, turning only once, or bake in a hot waffle iron. Serve hot with butter and syrup. YIELD: 12 pancakes or 8 waffles.

* See p 20 for alternatives to pancake mix.

Griddle Cakes

Sifted all-purpose flour	1¼ cups
Baking powder	1 tablespoon
Sugar	1 tablespoon
Salt	½ teaspoon
Milk	1¼ cups
Eggs, beaten	1
Butter, melted	¼ cup (½ stick)

Into a bowl sift together flour, baking powder, sugar and salt. In a small bowl beat together milk and egg; stir in butter. Add to dry ingredients and stir just until moistened (batter will be lumpy). Using ¼ cup measure, pour batter on to ungreased, preheated griddle. Bake until top is bubbly and edges baked. Turn and bake other side. Serve at once with butter and syrup. YIELD: 8 cakes.

VARIATION: *Buttermilk Griddle Cakes:* Follow above recipe except reduce baking powder to 2 teaspoons and add ½ teaspoon baking soda. Use 1¼ cups buttermilk in place of milk.

Easy Buttermilk Waffles

Buttermilk	1¾ cups
Eggs	1
Butter, melted	¼ cup
Baking soda	¼ teaspoon
Pancake mix*	1¾ cups

Place first three ingredients in bowl. Stir baking soda into pancake mix and add to mixture in bowl. Beat with rotary beater until fairly smooth. Bake on hot waffle iron until steaming stops. YIELD: 4 servings.

* See p 20 for alternatives to pancake mix.

Cornmeal Waffles

Sifted flour	$\frac{1}{2}$ cup
Baking powder	1 teaspoon
Salt	$\frac{1}{2}$ teaspoon
Sugar	1 tablespoon
Cornmeal	$\frac{1}{2}$ cup
Milk	$\frac{2}{3}$ cup
Butter, melted	$\frac{1}{4}$ cup
Eggs, separated	2

Mix and sift flour, baking powder, salt and sugar. Add cornmeal; stir in. Add milk and butter to beaten egg yolks. Add to dry ingredients all at once; mix well. Fold in stiffly beaten egg whites. Bake on hot waffle iron. Serve with butter and maple syrup. YIELD: 3 large waffles.

Apple Waffles

Milk	2 cups
Eggs	2
Pancake mix*	2 cups
Butter *or* margarine, melted	$\frac{1}{3}$ cup
Apples, chopped	1 cup (1 medium size apple)

Place milk, eggs, pancake mix and melted butter in bowl. Beat with rotary beater until batter is fairly smooth. Stir in apples. Bake in hot waffle baker until steaming stops. Serve with butter and cinnamon sugar. YIELD: serves 6.

* See p 20 for alternatives to pancake mix.

Apple Walnut Griddlecakes

Pancake mix*	2 cups
Sugar	1 tablespoon
Cinnamon	$\frac{1}{2}$ teaspoon

Apples, finely chopped	1 cup (1 medium size apple)
Walnuts, chopped	$\frac{1}{2}$ cup
Milk	$1\frac{3}{4}$ cups

Combine pancake mix, sugar and cinnamon. Stir in apples and walnuts. Add milk gradually. Bake on a hot griddle, turning when underside is golden brown and bubbles on top have 'set'. YIELD: 12 large griddlecakes.

* See p 20 for alternatives to pancake mix.

7

Pancakes

The worthy staple of the old pioneers is now a much-in-demand breakfast food. The pancake looks flat and humble, but it offers a hearty joy of good taste. Pancakes may be used as a dessert after a main course, too. There are few limits to the joys of good pancake eating.

Pleasing Pancakes

Flour	2 cups
Baking powder	4 teaspoons
Salt	1 teaspoon
Sugar	2 tablespoons
Eggs, well beaten	1
Milk	$1\frac{3}{4}$ cups
Oil *or* melted shortening	$\frac{1}{3}$ cup

Heat griddle while mixing batter. When griddle is hot enough, drops of water sprinkled on it will bounce. Mix dry ingredients thoroughly. Combine egg with milk and shortening. Add to dry ingredients and stir only until combined. Batter will be lumpy. For each pancake, pour about $\frac{1}{4}$ cup batter on to hot griddle. Cook until edges become slightly dry and bubbles form on top. Turn and brown the other side. YIELD: 12 pancakes, $4\frac{1}{2}$ in in diameter.

VARIATIONS: *Waffles:* Increase eggs to 3. Pour batter into hot waffle iron and bake until steaming has almost stopped. TIP: For a lighter-textured waffle, beat egg whites separately until stiff but not dry. Fold into waffle batter.

Sunshine Orange Pancakes

All-purpose biscuit mix*	1¾ cups
Milk	1½ cups
Eggs	1
Frozen orange juice concentrate, thawed, undiluted, divided	1 (6oz) can
Butter	½ cup
Sugar	1 cup

Combine biscuit mix, milk, egg and ¼ cup of the undiluted concentrate. Beat with rotary beater to combine. (Does not need to be completely smooth.) Bake pancakes on lightly greased griddle or in skillet. Turn once when bubbles appear. To prepare sauce, combine butter, sugar and remaining ½ cup undiluted concentrate in small saucepan. Heat to boiling. Serve slightly warm. YIELD: 18–20 medium pancakes; 1½ cups sauce.

* See p 20 for alternative to all-purpose biscuit mix.

Take-Your-Pick Pancakes

Pancake mix*	2 cups
Milk	2 cups
Eggs	2
Melted or liquid shortening	2 tablespoons

Nuts, chopped for sprinkling on pancakes
Seasonal berries for sprinkling on pancakes
Canned whole kernel corn, drained for sprinkling on pancakes
Chopped raw apple for sprinkling on pancakes

Place mix, milk, eggs and shortening in a bowl. Stir lightly until batter is fairly smooth. Pour batter on to hot, lightly greased griddle. Sprinkle each pancake with nutmeats, berries, corn or apples. Turn pancakes when tops are covered with bubbles and edges look cooked. Turn only once. Serve with butter and syrup. YIELD: Serves 8.

* See p 20 for alternatives to pancake mix.

German Apple Pancakes

Eggs	4
Sifted cake flour	½ cup
Salt	½ teaspoon
Sugar	¼ cup
Milk	½ cup
Lemon rind, grated	½ teaspoon
Lemon juice	1 tablespoon
Apple, coarsely grated	1 medium apple
Butter	2 tablespoons
Sour cream	½ cup

Beat egg yolks until light and fluffy. Now mix and sift flour, salt and sugar together. Add alternately with milk to egg mixture; mix well. Stir in lemon rind and juice. Fold in grated apple. Melt butter in 10in skillet. Pour in batter and bake at 400°F (hot oven) for 10 minutes. Reduce heat to 350°F (moderate oven). Bake an additional 15 minutes. Loosen sides and bottom of pancake immediately with spatula. Spread sour cream over half of the pancake. Cover with other half of pancake like an omelet. Remove to hot platter. TIP: Serve with apple or fresh fruit slices. YIELD: 4 servings.

Blueberry Pancakes

Sifted flour	1 cup
Baking powder	1½ teaspoons
Sugar	1 tablespoon
Salt	½ teaspoon
Cinnamon	¼ teaspoon

Butter, melted	2 tablespoons
Eggs, separated	1
Milk	¾ cup
Blueberries	¾ cup

Mix and sift flour, baking powder, sugar, salt and cinnamon. Add melted butter to beaten egg yolk. Stir in milk. Add to dry ingredients, mixing just enough to moisten. Fold in stiffly beaten egg white. Add berries and mix lightly. Bake on greased griddle. Serve with butter. YIELD: 8 large pancakes.

Buttermilk Pancakes Deluxe

Buttermilk	1¼ cups
Eggs, well beaten	2
Sifted flour	1 cup
Baking soda	½ teaspoon
Sugar	1 tablespoon
Salt	½ teaspoon
Butter, melted	¼ cup

Heat griddle very slowly. Add buttermilk to eggs; beat well with rotary beater. Add mixed and sifted flour, soda, sugar and salt. Beat until smooth. Add butter, mix in quickly. For each pancake, drop ¼ cup batter on a hot, lightly greased griddle and bake until brown on both sides, turning only once. YIELD: About 9 pancakes.

Light-as-a-Feather Pancakes

Eggs, separated	3
Salt	¼ teaspoon
Flour	¼ cup
Creamed cottage cheese	¾ cup

Heat griddle very slowly. Beat egg whites with egg beater until stiff but not dry. Now beat yolks with the same beater until light and lemon coloured. Stir in salt, flour and cheese. Fold in whites. Drop by small spoonfuls on hot, lightly greased griddle. Bake until golden brown on both sides. Serve immediately with butter and maple syrup. YIELD: 12 pancakes.

Quick 'n' Easy Buttermilk Pancakes

Buttermilk	2¼ cups
Eggs	1
Pancake mix*	2 cups
Baking soda	½ teaspoon
Shortening, melted	2 tablespoons

Place buttermilk and egg in bowl. Add pancake mix into which soda has been stirred. Mix lightly. Add melted shortening. Stir slightly. (Do not stir out small lumps.) For thinner pancakes, add about ¼ cup more buttermilk. Drop batter on hot, lightly greased griddle and bake until golden brown on both sides. YIELD: About 15 pancakes.

* See p 20 for alternative to pancake mix.

Appealing Pancakes

All-purpose buttermilk biscuit mix*	2 cups
Cinnamon	½ teaspoon
Eggs	1
Milk	1½ cups
Apple, grated	¾ cup (1 medium size apple)

Beat baking mix, cinnamon, egg and milk with rotary beater until smooth. Fold in apple. Pour batter from ¼ cup measuring cup on to hot griddle. (Grease griddle if necessary.) Bake until bubbles appear. Turn and bake other side until golden brown. YIELD: About 18.

* See p 20 for alternatives to all-purpose buttermilk biscuit mix.

Old-Fashioned Potato Pancakes

Shortening	¼ cup
Eggs	2
Milk	¼ cup
Finely shredded, un-cooked potatoes, well drained	2 cups
All-purpose butter-milk biscuit mix*	¼ cup
Salt	1 teaspoon

Melt shortening in large skillet. Beat eggs with rotary beater until fluffy; stir in remaining ingredients. Drop mixture by tablespoons into hot shortening. Cook about 3 minutes on each side or until golden brown. YIELD: About 18 pancakes.

* See p 20 for alternatives to all-purpose buttermilk biscuit mix.

Yeast Risen Pancakes

Sifted all-purpose flour	2 cups
Sugar	1 teaspoon
Active dry yeast *or*	1 package
Compressed yeast	1 cake
Warm milk (110°F)	1¼ cups
Eggs, separated	1
Salt	½ teaspoon

Mix in a large bowl, the flour, sugar, yeast and warm milk to a batter. Cover bowl and let stand until the batter is bubbly (20 to 30 minutes). Add egg yolk and stir in. Whisk egg white until stiff, stir in salt and fold into batter. Pour batter from a tablespoon on to lightly greased, hot griddle. Bake until bubbles appear. Turn and bake other side until golden brown. When cooked, turn on to sugared greaseproof paper. Serve piled in threes, sandwiched together with fruit sauce or fruit jam, sliced fruit or butter. YIELD: 15 pancakes.

French Pancakes

Sifted all-purpose flour	1 cup
Salt	$\frac{1}{4}$ teaspoon
Eggs	1
Milk	$1\frac{1}{4}$ cups
Fat or oil for frying	
Sugar ⎫	for serving
Lemon juice ⎭	

Sift together the flour and salt. Make a well in centre, and add beaten egg and half the milk. Stir the flour in gradually, avoid lumps forming, and add more milk when necessary to mix easily. Beat well until smooth and then add and stir in the remainder of the milk. Heat a little fat or oil in a skillet, frying or omelet pan. When hot, pour or spoon in just enough batter to cover the base of the pan thinly and cook quickly until golden brown underneath. Turn with a palette knife or toss and allow to brown on the other side. Turn out on to sugared paper, sprinkle with lemon juice and more sugar and roll up. Keep in a warm place covered while the rest of the pancakes are cooked. Serve with lemon wedges. YIELD: 6–8.

Stack 'em High Hotcakes

Bran flakes	$\frac{1}{2}$ cup
Milk	1 cup
Butter or margarine, melted	3 tablespoons
Eggs, beaten	1
Sifted all-purpose flour	1 cup

Baking powder   2½ teaspoons
Granulated sugar   3 tablespoons
Salt   ¾ teaspoon
Maple syrup for serving

Soak bran flakes in milk for 5 minutes. Stir in butter or margarine and egg. Beat lightly. Sift together next four ingredients. Stir into bran mixture until blended. Cook on greased griddle, browning on both sides. Serve with maple syrup. YIELD: About 16 (3in) pancakes.

Cheese Pancakes

Milk   1 cup
Butter *or* margarine   2 tablespoons
Bread crumbs   1½ cups
Eggs, beaten   3
All-purpose flour   ½ cup
Baking powder   1½ table-
                             spoons
Salt   ¼ teaspoon
Cheddar cheese,
  grated   ½ cup

In medium saucepan, scald milk; add butter or margarine; stir until melted. Add bread crumbs. Let stand until soft. Add eggs and mix well. Sift together next three ingredients; stir into batter with cheese. Cook on greased griddle, browning on both sides. YIELD: About 12 (4in) pancakes.

8

No-Knead Breads

No time to knead? There are many deliciously good yeast recipes that do not require any kneading. Some of the great classics are knead-less doughs. The batter is just mixed, allowed to rise . . . and then baked. Simple, yes. Delicious—oh, yes!!!

No-Knead Batter Bread

Active dry yeast	1 package
or	
Compressed yeast	1 cake
Warm water	$\frac{1}{4}$ cup
Milk	1 cup
Sugar	$\frac{1}{4}$ cup
Eggs	1
Salt	1 teaspoon
Oil or soft shortening	$\frac{1}{4}$ cup
Sifted all-purpose flour	$3\frac{1}{4}$ cups

Dissolve the yeast in warm water. Add scalded milk to sugar, salt and oil or soft shortening. Cool to lukewarm. Add 2 cups of flour. Beat well with a spoon or mix 1 minute on medium-low speed of mixer. Add dissolved yeast and egg. Beat well again with spoon or 1 minute medium-low speed of mixer. Add remaining flour to make a thick batter. Beat until smooth. Cover and let rise in a warm place, 80°F to 85°F, until doubled in size. Stir down and smooth into two greased 8 × 8 × 2in pans. Cover and let rise until almost doubled (about 50 minutes). Bake at 375°F (moderate oven) for 25 to 35 minutes.

NOTE: When you use topping, the baking time is usually about 35 minutes. YIELD: 2 loaves.

Golden Yellow No-Knead Bread

Active dry yeast	1 package
or	
Compressed yeast	1 cake
Warm water	$\frac{1}{4}$ cup
Butter	$\frac{1}{3}$ cup
Sugar	$\frac{1}{3}$ cup
Salt	$\frac{1}{2}$ teaspoon
Boiling water	$\frac{1}{2}$ cup
Evaporated milk	$\frac{3}{4}$ cup
Eggs, beaten	2
Sifted all-purpose flour	$4\frac{1}{2}$ cups

Sprinkle dry yeast over warm water; set aside for 10 minutes or dissolve fresh yeast in warm water. In a mixing bowl combine butter, sugar and salt; add boiling water and stir until butter is melted. Stir in evaporated milk, eggs and dissolved yeast. Beat in flour, 1 cup at a time, beating until fairly smooth after each addition. Cover and let stand in warm place until doubled (1–1$\frac{1}{2}$ hours). Beat batter down, then beat for 4 minutes with a wooden spoon. Turn into buttered 10in tube pan. Cover and let stand in warm place until doubled (about 45 minutes). Bake 45 minutes in preheated 350°F (moderate) oven. Turn out immediately on to wire rack and cool, right side up. YIELD: 1 loaf.

VARIATION: *Rolls:* After beating dough down, spoon into well-buttered muffin cups, filling each cup half full. Cover and let stand in warm place until doubled (30 to 45 minutes). Bake 20 to 30 minutes. Makes 18 rolls.

No-Knead Rolls (Cottage Style)

Unsifted all-purpose flour	3–4 cups
Sugar	$\frac{1}{3}$ cup
Salt	1 teaspoon

Active dry yeast	1 package
or	
Compressed yeast	1 cake
Water, warm	
(110°F)	¼ cup
Milk	½ cup
Margarine	½ cup (1 stick)
Eggs	3
Egg yolk	1
Egg white, lightly	
beaten	1
Sugar	1 tablespoon

In a large bowl thoroughly mix 1 cup flour, ⅓ cup sugar, salt, undissolved or crumbled yeast and warm water. Put aside for 20 minutes until bubbly. Place milk and margarine in a saucepan. Heat over low heat until milk is very warm (120–30°F). Margarine does not need to melt. Now gradually add to flour and yeast mix and beat 2 minutes at medium speed of electric mixer, scraping bowl occasionally. Add eggs, egg yolk and ¾ cup flour. Beat at high speed 2 minutes, scraping bowl occasionally. Stir in enough additional flour to make a soft dough. Cover; let rise in a warm place, until more than doubled in bulk, about 2 hours. Stir down. Cover bowl tightly with aluminium foil and refrigerate overnight. Next day punch dough down; turn out on to lightly floured board. Divide into 2 pieces, one about ¾ of the dough and the other ¼ of the dough. Cut larger piece into 24 equal pieces. Form into small balls. Place in well greased 2½ × 1¼ in muffin pans. Cut smaller pieces into 24 equal pieces; form into smooth balls. Make a deep indentation in centre of each large ball; dampen slightly with cold water. Press a small ball into each indentation. Cover; let rise in a warm place, free from draught, until doubled in bulk, about 50 minutes. Combine egg white and 1 tablespoon sugar; carefully brush over rolls. Bake at 375°F (moderate oven) for about 15 minutes or until done. Remove from pans and cool on wire racks. YIELD: About 24 rolls.

No-Knead Banana Batter Bread

Unsifted flour	2½–3 cups
Sugar	⅓ cup
Salt	¾ teaspoon
Baking soda	½ teaspoon
Ground cinnamon	½ teaspoon
Active dry yeast *or*	1 package
Compressed yeast	1 cake
Milk	¼ cup
Water	¼ cup
Margarine	3 tablespoons
Eggs	1
Ripe bananas, mashed	⅔ cup (2 large bananas)
Peanuts *or* pecans, chopped	½ cup

In a large bowl, thoroughly mix ½ cup flour, sugar, salt, soda, cinnamon and crumbled fresh yeast or undissolved yeast. Put aside. Combine milk, water and margarine in a saucepan. Heat over low heat until liquids are very warm (120–30°F). Margarine does not need to melt. Gradually add to dry ingredients and beat 2 minutes at medium speed of electric mixer, scraping bowl occasionally. Add egg, bananas and ¼ cup flour. Beat at high speed 2 minutes, scraping bowl occasionally. Add pecans and enough additional flour to make a soft dough. Cover; let rise in warm place, free from draught, until doubled in bulk, about 1 hour. Stir down; turn into 2 greased 7½ × 3¾ × 2¼in loaf pans. Cover; let rise in warm place, free from draught, until doubled in bulk, about 1 hour. Bake at 375°F (moderate oven) for about 35 minutes or until done. Remove from pans and cool on wire racks. YIELD: 2 small loaves.

No-Knead Lemon Spice Muffins

Milk	¾ cup
Sugar	6 tablespoons
Salt	1 teaspoon
Margarine	5 tablespoons
Grated lemon peel	1 tablespoon
Lemon juice	1 teaspoon
Warm water (105–15°F)	¼ cup
Active dry yeast *or*	1 package
Compressed yeast	1 cake
Eggs, beaten	3
Unsifted flour	3 cups
Sugar	1 tablespoon
Cinnamon	1 teaspoon

Scald milk; stir in 6 tablespoons sugar, salt, margarine, lemon peel and lemon juice. Cool to lukewarm. Measure warm water into large bowl. Sprinkle or crumble in yeast; stir until dissolved. Add lukewarm milk mixture and eggs. Blend in flour, 1 cup at a time. Beat until smooth. Cover; let rise in a warm place, free from draught, until doubled in bulk, about 1 hour. Stir batter down. Fill greased muffin cups about half full. Sprinkle with mixture of 1 tablespoon sugar and cinnamon. Cover; let rise in warm place, free from draught, until doubled, about 45 minutes. Bake at 375°F (moderate oven) for about 20 minutes or until done. YIELD: About 18 muffins.

No-Knead Egg Casserole Bread

Unsifted flour	5½–6½ cups
Sugar	2 tablespoons
Salt	1 tablespoon
Active dry yeast *or*	2 packages
Compressed yeast	2 cakes
Softened margarine	2 tablespoons

| Warm water (120–30°F) | 2 cups |
| Eggs (at room temperature) | **3** |

In a large bowl thoroughly mix 1½ cups flour, sugar, salt and undissolved yeast. Add margarine. Gradually add warm water to dry ingredients and beat 2 minutes at medium speed of electric mixer, scraping bowl occasionally. Add eggs and ½ cup flour. Beat at high speed 2 minutes, scraping bowl occasionally. Stir in enough additional flour to make a soft dough. Cover; let rise in warm place, free from draught, until doubled in bulk, about 35 minutes. Stir down; turn into 2 greased 1½ quart casseroles. Cover; let rise in warm place, free from draught, until doubled in bulk, about 40 minutes. Bake at 375°F (moderate oven) for about 35 minutes or until done. Remove from casseroles and cool on wire racks. YIELD: 2 loaves.

No-Knead Herb Sour Cream Bread

Warm water (105–15°F)	½ cup
Active dry yeast *or*	2 packages
Compressed yeast	2 cakes
Dairy sour cream, warm	1 cup
Softened margarine	6 tablespoons
Sugar	⅓ cup
Salt	2 teaspoons
Marjoram leaves	½ teaspoon
Oregano leaves	½ teaspoon
Thyme leaves	½ teaspoon
Eggs (at room temperature)	2
Unsifted flour	3¾–4¾ cups

Measure warm water into large, warm bowl. Sprinkle or crumble in yeast; stir until dissolved and leave to stand for 10 minutes. Add sour cream, margarine, sugar, salt, marjoram, oregano, thyme and eggs. Beat in 3 cups flour until well blended, about 1 minute. Stir in enough additional flour to make a soft dough. Cover; let rise in warm place, free from draught, until doubled in bulk, about 50 minutes. Stir down. Turn into 2 greased 1 quart casseroles. Cover; let rise in warm place, free from draught, until doubled in bulk, about 50 minutes. Bake at 375°F (moderate) for about 35 minutes or until done. Remove from casseroles and cool on wire racks. YIELD: 2 loaves.

No-Knead Garlic Casserole Breads

Warm water (105–15°F)	1 cup
Active dry yeast *or*	2 packages
Compressed yeast	2 cakes
Warm milk	1 cup
Softened margarine	2 tablespoons
Sugar	3 tablespoons
Salt	1 tablespoon
Instant minced garlic, reconstituted*	$\frac{1}{2}$ teaspoon
Unsifted flour	$4\frac{1}{2}$–$5\frac{1}{2}$ cups
Egg white	1
Cold water	1 tablespoon
Parmesan cheese, grated	
Paprika	

Measure warm water into large warm bowl. Sprinkle or crumble in yeast; stir until dissolved and leave to stand for 10 minutes. Add milk, margarine, sugar, salt and garlic. Beat in 3 cups flour until well blended, about 1 minute. Stir in enough additional flour to make a soft dough; cover. Let rise in warm place, free from draught, until doubled in bulk, about 35 minutes. Stir down. Spoon evenly into 6 greased, 10oz, deep pie dishes or 24 greased muffin pans, $2\frac{1}{2} \times 1\frac{1}{4}$in. Cover. Let rise in warm place, free from draught, until doubled in bulk, about 35 minutes. Combine egg white and cold water. Carefully brush loaves or rolls with egg mixture. Sprinkle with cheese and paprika. Bake at 375°F (moderate) for about 35 minutes for loaves, 25 minutes for rolls, or until done. Remove from dishes or pans and cool on wire racks. YIELD: 6 small loaves or 24 rolls.

* 1 teaspoon instant minced garlic is equivalent to 1 tablespoon finely chopped fresh onion.

No-Knead Poppy Seed Batter Bread

Warm water (105–15°F)	1¼ cups
Active dry yeast *or*	1 package
Compressed yeast	1 cake
Softened margarine	2 tablespoons
Poppy seeds	2 tablespoons
Sugar	2 tablespoons
Salt	2 tablespoons
Unsifted flour	3–3½ cups
Egg white	1
Cold water	1 tablespoon
Poppy seeds for sprinkling top of loaf	

Measure warm water into large warm bowl. Sprinkle or crumble in yeast; stir until dissolved and leave to stand for 10 minutes. Add margarine, 2 tablespoons poppy seeds, sugar and salt. Stir in 2 cups flour. Beat until well blended, about 1 minute. Stir in enough additional flour to make a soft dough. Cover; let rise in warm place, free from draught, until doubled in bulk, about 35 minutes. Stir down. Spread evenly in greased 9 × 5 × 3in loaf pan. Cover; let rise in warm place, free from draught, until doubled in bulk, about 40 minutes. Combine egg white and cold water; carefully brush on top of loaf. Sprinkle with poppy seeds. Bake at 375°F (moderate) for about 45 minutes, or until done. Remove from pan and cool on wire rack. YIELD: 1 loaf.

No-Knead Casserole Swedish Rye Bread

Unsifted white flour	3½–4 cups
Unsifted rye flour	1½ cups
Dark brown sugar	⅓ cup firmly packed
Salt	2 teaspoons
Caraway seeds	1 teaspoon
Active dry yeast *or*	2 packages
Compressed yeast	2 cakes
Milk	1 cup
Water	1 cup
Margarine	2 tablespoons

Combine flours. In a large bowl, thoroughly mix 1½ cups flour mixture, sugar, salt, caraway seeds and undissolved dry yeast. Combine milk, water and margarine in saucepan. Heat over low heat until liquids are very warm (120–30°F). Margarine does not need to melt. Gradually add to dry ingredients and beat 2 minutes at medium speed of electric mixer, scraping bowl occasionally. Add ¾ cup flour mixture. Beat at high speed 2 minutes, scraping bowl occasionally. Stir in enough additional flour mixture to make a stiff dough. (If necessary, use additional white flour to obtain desired dough.) Cover; let rise in warm place, free from draught, until doubled in bulk, about 40 minutes. Stir dough down. Cover; let rise again until doubled in bulk, about 20 minutes. Stir down; turn into a well-greased 1½ quart casserole. Bake at 400°F (hot oven) for about 40 minutes or until done. Remove from casserole and cool on wire rack. YIELD: 1 loaf.

No-Knead Easy-to-Make Bread

Warm water (105–15°F)	½ cup
Active dry yeast *or*	1 package
Compressed yeast	1 cake

Warm milk	1 cup
Softened margarine	$\frac{1}{2}$ cup (1 stick)
Sugar	$\frac{1}{4}$ cup
Salt	2 teaspoons
Eggs, well beaten	3
Unsifted flour	$5\frac{1}{2}$–6 cups

Measure warm water into large warm bowl. Sprinkle or crumble in yeast; stir until dissolved and leave to stand for 10 minutes. Add milk, margarine, sugar, salt and eggs. Stir in 3 cups flour. Beat until well blended, about 1 minute. Stir in enough remaining flour to make a soft dough. Cover; let rise in warm place, free from draught, until doubled in bulk, about 1 hour. Stir down; spoon into well-greased and floured 10in baking pan or 2 well-greased 9 × 5 × 3in loaf pans. Cover; let rise in warm place, free from draught, until doubled in bulk, about 1 hour. Bake large loaf at 400°F (hot oven) for about 30 minutes or until done. Bake small loaves at 375°F (moderate) for about 30 minutes or until done. Remove from pans and cool on wire racks. YIELD: 1 large or 2 small loaves.

9

Quick Breads

If you're pressed for time, whether by job or household duties, try the new, quick bread way of baking. You use a packaged mix, but you give the recipe a little something extra in the way of personally selected ingredients. The result? A quick bread that has something of the good, old-fashioned taste of home-made bread.

Quick Nut Loaf

Sifted flour	2½ cups
Sugar	2 tablespoons
Baking powder	3 teaspoons
Salt	½ teaspoon
Cinnamon	½ teaspoon
Milk	1 cup
Eggs, beaten	2
Melted shortening *or* oil	4 tablespoons
Chopped nuts	1 cup

Sift together flour, sugar, baking powder, salt and cinnamon. Add milk to eggs. Stir into dry ingredients and mix just until smooth. Stir in the shortening and nuts. Pour into a greased loaf pan. Let stand 20 minutes. Bake at 350°F (moderate oven) for about 1 hour. YIELD: 1 loaf.

VARIATION: *Raisin Loaf:* Use 1½ cups chopped raisins instead of nuts.

Fruit Nut Bread

Dried apricots	½ cup
Raisins	½ cup
Water	¾ cup
Grated orange rind	½ teaspoon
Orange juice	¼ cup
Baking soda	1 teaspoon
Sugar	¾ cup
Melted shortening *or* oil	2 tablespoons
Vanilla	1 teaspoon
Eggs, beaten	1
Sifted flour	2½ cups
Baking powder	4 teaspoons
Salt	¼ teaspoon
Chopped nuts	½ cup

Soak apricots and raisins in the water for 30 minutes. Drain; save the liquid. Chop the fruit fine. Add orange rind, juice and drained liquid to the fruit. Stir in the soda, sugar, shortening, vanilla and egg. Sift together the flour, baking powder and salt. Combine with the fruit mixture. Add the nuts and blend well. Pour into a greased loaf pan. Bake at 350°F (moderate oven) for about 1 hour. YIELD: 1 large loaf.

Cranberry Orange Bread

All-purpose biscuit mix*	3 cups
Grated orange rind	1 tablespoon
Sugar	¾ cup
Baking soda	¼ teaspoon
Soft butter *or* margarine	2 tablespoons
Eggs, beaten	1
Milk	¾ cup
Orange juice	½ cup

| Chopped nuts | ½ cup |
| Fresh cranberries, coarsely chopped | 1 cup |

Combine biscuit mix, orange rind, sugar, baking soda and butter in large bowl. Mix together beaten egg, milk and orange juice. Add to biscuit mixture and beat well for about 1 minute. Stir in nuts and cranberries. Spoon into well-greased 9 × 5 × 3in loaf pan. Bake in 350°F (moderate) oven for 55 to 60 minutes. Let stand in pan 10 minutes. Turn out on rack to cool. Wrap in saran film or aluminium foil and store overnight before slicing. YIELD: 1 loaf.

VARIATIONS: *Orange-Raisin Bread:* Substitute ¾ cup raisins for the cranberries.

Apricot Bread: Substitute 1 cup finely cut-up, uncooked dried apricots for the cranberries.

* See p 20 for alternative to all-purpose biscuit mix.

Florida Fruit Bread

Sugar	1½ cups
Water	⅓ cup
Orange peel, slivered	¾ cup (about 4 oranges)
Butter *or* margarine	¼ cup
Orange juice	1½ cups
Eggs, beaten	2
Sifted all-purpose flour	4 cups
Baking powder	4 teaspoons
Baking soda	½ teaspoon
Salt	2 teaspoons

Combine sugar and water in saucepan. Add peel and stir constantly over medium heat until sugar is dissolved. Reduce heat and cook slowly for 5 minutes. The peel and syrup should measure 1½ cups. Add butter; stir until melted. Cool; then add orange juice and beaten eggs. Sift dry ingredients together in mixing bowl. Add liquid mixture to flour mixture and stir until flour is dampened. Turn batter into two greased 8½ × 4½ × 2½in pans. Bake at 325°F (slow oven) for 45 to 50 minutes. Let stand in pans 10 minutes. Turn out on rack to cool. YIELD: 2 loaves.

Easy Date Nut Bread

All-purpose sifted flour	2½ cups
Sugar	1 cup
Baking powder	3½ teaspoons
Salt	1 teaspoon
Salad oil	3 tablespoons
Milk	1¼ cups
Eggs	1
Chopped nuts	1 cup
Dates, chopped	1 cup

Heat oven to 350°F (moderate oven). Grease and flour loaf pan, 9 × 5 × 3in. Measure all ingredients into large mixer bowl; beat on medium speed ½ minute. Pour into prepared pan. Bake 55 to 65 minutes or until wooden tester inserted in centre comes out clean. Cool thoroughly before slicing. YIELD: 1 loaf.

VARIATIONS: *Apricot-Nut Bread*: Follow preceding recipe except—reduce milk to ½ cup; omit the dates and add 4 teaspoons grated orange peel, ¾ cup orange juice and 1 cup finely chopped dried apricots.

Nut Rolls: Follow preceding recipe except—divide batter equally among 10 (6oz) frozen juice cans. Bake about 40 minutes or until wooden tester inserted in centre comes out clean.

Fluffy Spoonbread

Boiling water	1½ cups
Cornmeal	1 cup
Butter *or* margarine, softened	1 tablespoon

Eggs, separated	3
Buttermilk	1 cup
Salt	1 teaspoon
Sugar	1 teaspoon
Baking powder	1 teaspoon
Soda	$\frac{1}{4}$ teaspoon

Heat oven to 375°F (moderate). Grease a 2 quart casserole. In a large bowl, stir boiling water into cornmeal; continue stirring to prevent lumping until cool. Blend in 1 tablespoon butter and the egg yolks. Stir in buttermilk, salt, sugar, baking powder and soda. Beat egg whites *just* until soft peaks form; fold into batter. Pour into prepared casserole. Bake 45 to 50 minutes. Serve not with butter. YIELD: Serves 6.

Oatmeal Nut Bread

Eggs	2
Sugar	1 cup
Buttermilk	2 cups
Molasses	$\frac{2}{3}$ cup
Sifted all-purpose flour	3 cups
Baking soda	2 teaspoons
Baking powder	1 teaspoon
Salt	1 teaspoon
Quick-cooking rolled oats	$1\frac{1}{2}$ cups
Nuts, chopped	$1\frac{1}{2}$ cups
Dates, chopped	$1\frac{1}{2}$ cups

In a mixing bowl, beat eggs until light; gradually add sugar, beating constantly. Blend in buttermilk and molasses. Sift together flour, baking soda, baking powder and salt; gradually add to buttermilk mixture, beating only until blended. Stir in just enough rolled oats, nuts and dates to combine evenly. Divide into 2 buttered loaf pans, $8\frac{1}{2} \times 4\frac{1}{2} \times 2\frac{1}{2}$ in. Bake in preheated 350°F (moderate) oven for 50 to 60 minutes. Turn out of pans on to wire rack to cool. TIP: Bread will slice better on second day. YIELD: 2 loaves.

Sour Cream Nut Bread

Eggs	1
Light brown sugar	1 cup, firmly packed
Dairy sour cream	1 cup
Sifted all-purpose flour	2 cups
Baking powder	1 teaspoon
Baking soda	1 teaspoon
Salt	1 teaspoon
Cinnamon	$\frac{1}{4}$ teaspoon
Nutmeg	$\frac{1}{4}$ teaspoon
Ground cloves	$\frac{1}{4}$ teaspoon
Nuts, chopped	1 cup

In a mixing bowl, beat egg; add sugar and mix well. Carefully stir in sour cream. Sift together flour, baking powder, baking soda, salt, cinnamon, nutmeg and cloves; add to cream mixture, stirring just until moistened. Add nuts. Turn into buttered loaf pan, $8\frac{1}{2} \times 4\frac{1}{2} \times 2\frac{1}{2}$in. Bake in preheated 350°F (moderate) oven, 50 to 60 minutes. Turn out of pan on to wire rack to cool. Slice while warm or after completely cooled. YIELD: 1 loaf.

Banana Nut Bread

Butter	$\frac{1}{2}$ cup (1 stick)
Sugar	$\frac{1}{2}$ cup
Eggs	2
Bananas, mashed	$1\frac{1}{2}$ cups (about 3 bananas)
Walnuts, chopped	$\frac{1}{2}$ cup
Sifted all-purpose flour	2 cups
Baking powder	$\frac{1}{2}$ teaspoon
Baking soda	$\frac{1}{2}$ teaspoon
Salt	$\frac{1}{2}$ teaspoon

In a mixing bowl, cream butter, gradually add sugar and beat until light and fluffy. Beat in eggs, one at a time. Blend in bananas and nuts. Sift together flour, baking powder, baking soda and salt. Gradually add to creamed mixture, beating only until blended. Turn into buttered loaf pan, 9 × 5 × 3in. Bake in preheated 350°F (moderate) oven, for 45 to 50 minutes. Cool in pan on wire rack 10 minutes; turn out of pan to complete cooling. YIELD: 1 loaf.

Easy Corn Bread

Sifted all-purpose flour	1 cup
Yellow cornmeal	1 cup
Sugar	3 tablespoons
Baking powder	1 tablespoon
Salt	1 teaspoon
Eggs	1
Milk	1 cup
Butter, melted	¼ cup (½ stick)

In a bowl combine flour, cornmeal, sugar, baking powder and salt. Beat together egg and milk; stir in butter. Add to dry ingredients, stirring just until moistened. Turn into buttered square pan, 8in. Bake at preheated 425°F (hot oven) for 25 minutes or until golden brown. Cut into squares. YIELD: Serves 9.

VARIATIONS: *Cheese Corn Bread:* Add 1 cup shredded Cheddar cheese to dry ingredients.

Corny Corn Bread: Reduce milk to ½ cup. Add 1 can (12oz) whole kernel corn with red and green sweet peppers, undrained, to dry ingredients, then add liquid ingredients.

Corn Bread Sticks: Prepare batter as for corn bread. Divide into buttered corn stick pans, filling each ⅔ full. Bake 15 to 18 minutes or until golden brown. Makes 18 sticks.

Fresh Orange Bread

Shortening	$\frac{1}{4}$ cup
Clear honey	1 cup
Eggs	1
Grated orange peel	$1\frac{1}{2}$ table-spoons
Sifted all-purpose flour	$2\frac{1}{2}$ cups
Baking powder	$2\frac{1}{2}$ teaspoons
Salt	1 teaspoon
Fresh orange juice	$\frac{3}{4}$ cup
Walnuts, finely chopped	$\frac{3}{4}$ cup

Cream shortening; continue creaming while adding honey in a fine stream. Add egg and beat well; add orange peel. Sift flour once, measure; add baking powder and salt and sift together. Add flour alternately with orange juice, a small amount at a time to first mixture, beating after each addition until smooth. Stir in nuts; blend. Turn into 9 × 5 × 3in lined, greased loaf pan; bake at 325°F (slow oven) for 1 hour or until done. Let cool in pan 10 minutes; then turn out of pan and let stand until cold. Wrap in waxed paper or aluminium foil. Store overnight to blend flavors and for easy slicing. YIELD: 1 loaf.

Lemon Drop Bread

Butter	$\frac{1}{4}$ cup
Sugar	$\frac{1}{3}$ cup
Eggs	1
Milk	1 cup
Lemon juice	1 tablespoon
Packaged biscuit mix*	2 cups
Lemon Topping:	
Sugar	$\frac{1}{3}$ cup
Grated lemon rind	2 teaspoons
Butter, melted	1 teaspoon

Cream butter; add sugar gradually; continue to cream until light and fluffy. Add egg; beat well. Add biscuit mix, then milk; stir quickly until just blended. Add lemon juice; stir in. Now pour into well-buttered, square baking pan, 8 × 8 × 2in. Mix lemon topping ingredients with a fork. Sprinkle on top. Bake in hot oven, 400°F, 30 to 40 minutes. Cut into squares. Especially delicious warm. YIELD: 9 squares.

* See pp 19–20 for alternative to packaged biscuit mix.

Berry Bread

Sifted all-purpose flour	2 cups
Granulated sugar	¾ cup
Baking powder	3 teaspoons
Salt	1 teaspoon
Baking soda	½ teaspoon
Cinnamon	1 teaspoon
Walnuts, chopped	1 cup
Eggs	1
Cranberry sauce	1 cup
Shortening, melted	2 tablespoons

Heat oven to 350°F (moderate oven). Sift together on to waxed paper the flour, sugar, baking powder, salt, soda and cinnamon. Add walnuts. In mixing bowl, beat egg; add cranberry sauce and shortening. Add dry ingredients; stir until just blended. Pour into greased 9 × 5 × 3in loaf pan. Bake at 350°F (moderate oven) for 45 minutes. Cool on rack. YIELD: 1 large loaf. TIP: 1 teaspoon grated lemon rind may also be added. Use remaining ½ cup cranberry sauce to blend with 1 package cream cheese. Use as a spread for tea sandwiches.

Old-Fashioned Berry Nut Loaf

Sifted flour	2 cups
Double acting baking powder	1½ teaspoons
Salt	1 teaspoon
Baking soda	½ teaspoon
Eggs, beaten	1
Orange juice	¾ cup
Water	¼ cup
Cooking oil	¼ cup
Cranberries, coarsely chopped	1 cup
Nuts, chopped	½ cup

Sift flour, measure; resift with baking powder, salt and soda. Combine beaten egg with orange juice, water and cooking oil. Stir into dry ingredients just enough to moisten. Fold in cranberries and nuts. Turn into well greased 9 × 5 × 3in pan. Bake at 350°F (moderate oven) for 50 to 60 minutes. YIELD: 1 large loaf.

Orange Prune Nut Loaf

Orange, medium sized	1
Baking soda	1 teaspoon
Fresh orange juice, heated to boiling	½ cup
Sugar	⅔ cup
Eggs	1
Butter *or* margarine, melted	1 tablespoon
Vanilla	½ teaspoon
Sifted flour	2 cups
Baking powder	2½ teaspoons
Salt	½ teaspoon
Pitted prunes, chopped	1 cup
Pecans *or* walnuts, chopped	1 cup

Put orange through food grinder. Sprinkle baking soda on top. Add hot orange juice stirring until blended. Set aside. In large mixing bowl, combine sugar, egg, melted butter and vanilla. Blend until smooth. Sift together flour, baking powder and salt. Add to creamed mixture all at once along with orange purée. Stir until batter is thoroughly blended. Add prunes and nuts. Batter is thick, so it will be necessary to stir, then partially fold and cut in order to mix evenly. Pour into greased 9 × 5 × 3in loaf pan. Bake at 300°F (slow oven) for 1 hour 10 minutes, or until loaf is done. Let stand in pan 5 minutes before turning out on to wire rack. When completely cool, wrap tightly in saran wrap or foil and store overnight in refrigerator to 'ripen'. YIELD: 1 large loaf.

Cheese Herb Bread

Sifted self-rising flour	2 cups
Salt	1½ teaspoons
Dry mustard	1 teaspoon
Mixed dried herbs	1 teaspoon
Fresh parsley, chopped	1 tablespoon
Cheddar cheese, grated	¾ cup
Eggs, beaten	1
Water	⅔ cup
Butter *or* margarine, melted	2 tablespoons

Sift flour, salt and mustard together and stir in the mixed herbs, parsley and grated cheese. Add the well-beaten egg, water and melted fat to the dry ingredients and stir until just blended. Spoon mixture into three well-greased soup cans or into a greased 8 × 4in loaf pan. Bake at 375°F (moderate) for about 45 minutes. Remove from cans or pan and cool. Serve freshly baked with butter and salad. YIELD: 3 small or 1 large loaf.

Farmhouse Malt Bread

Malt extract	¼ cup
Brown sugar	¼ cup, packed
Butter	2 tablespoons
Graham flour	2 cups less 2 tablespoons
Baking powder	2 teaspoons
Salt	¼ teaspoon
Milk	⅔ cup
Currants	⅓ cup
Sultanas	⅓ cup
Candied peel, chopped	2 tablespoons

Warm the malt extract, sugar and butter together stirring until the sugar and butter are dissolved and well blended. Allow to cool a little. Place the flour, baking powder and salt in a bowl and mix. Pour in the malt mixture and milk and mix thoroughly. Stir in the fruit and peel. Pour into a greased 1lb loaf pan and bake in a preheated oven, 325°F (slow oven) for 1¼ to 1½ hours. Delicious served with butter or cream cheese. YIELD: 1 loaf.

Cherry Nut Bread

All-purpose buttermilk biscuit mix*	3 cups
Sugar	½ cup
Sifted all-purpose flour	⅓ cup
Ground cardamom	1 teaspoon
Eggs	1
Milk	1 cup
Candied cherries, cut up	1 cup
Nuts, chopped	¾ cup

Preheat oven to 350°F (moderate). Meanwhile, combine baking mix, sugar, flour, cardamom, egg and milk; beat vigorously ½ minute. Stir in cherries and nuts. Pour batter into greased loaf pan, 9 × 5 × 3in. Bake up to 60 minutes or until wooden tester inserted in centre comes out clean. Cool thoroughly before slicing. YIELD: 1 large loaf.

* See p 20 for alternative to all-purpose buttermilk biscuit mix.

Cheese Flavored Dinner Bread

All-purpose butter-milk biscuit mix*	2 cups
Hard-boiled eggs, chopped	1 cup (4 eggs)
Instant minced onion	3 tablespoons
Eggs	2
Milk	⅔ cup
Salad oil	2 tablespoons
Cheddar cheese, grated	1½ cups
Sesame seeds	2 tablespoons
Butter *or* margarine, melted	3 tablespoons

Preheat oven to 375°F (moderate). Meanwhile, combine baking mix, chopped eggs, onion, 2 eggs, milk, oil and ¾ cup of the cheese; mix thoroughly. Spread the dough in a greased 10in pie pan. Sprinkle with remaining cheese and sesame seeds. Pour butter evenly over top. Bake up to 40 minutes. Cut into wedges. Serve warm. YIELD: 6 to 8 servings. TIP: Bread may be baked in greased square pan, 9 × 9 × 2in. Bake at 400°F (hot oven) for 35 to 40 minutes.

* See p 20 for alternative to all-purpose buttermilk biscuit mix.

Instant Onion Bread

All-purpose butter- milk biscuit mix*	2 cups
Cold water	½ cup
Instant minced onion	1 tablespoon
Soft butter *or* margarine	1 tablespoon
Poppy seeds for sprinkling on top of loaf	

Preheat oven to 450°F (very hot oven). Meanwhile, stir baking mix, water and onion to a soft dough. Roll dough on greased baking sheet into an oblong, 10 × 8in. Spread oblong with butter and sprinkle with poppy seeds. Bake 10 minutes. Serve hot. YIELD: 6 servings.

* See p 20 for alternative to all-purpose buttermilk biscuit mix.

10

Yeast Breads and Rolls

The traditional home-baked breads and rolls were made with yeast. Today, thanks to improved cooking methods, you can make these same old-fashioned baked goods in less time, with less effort, but with all the sheer goodness of those bygone days of yeast-rising breads.

Basic White Bread

Sifted all-purpose flour	6 cups
Milk	1¾ cups
Warm water (105–15°F)	¼ cup
Active dry yeast *or*	1 package
Compressed yeast	1 cake
Sugar	5 tablespoons
Salt	2 teaspoons
Cooking oil *or* shortening, melted	¼ cup

Scald milk and pour over the sugar, salt and oil or soft shortening which you have measured into a mixing bowl. Add half of the flour and beat well. Dissolve the yeast in ¼ cup of warm water. Add it to the batter and beat until smooth. Add the remainder of flour, or enough to make a moderately soft dough, and mix thoroughly.

Turn the dough out on a lightly floured board or pastry cloth. Knead it until it is smooth and elastic. Place the dough in a greased bowl: cover and let rise at 80°F to 85°F until doubled in bulk (about 1 hour and 20 minutes). Punch it down. Let it stand covered on the bread board for 5 minutes. Divide the dough in half and shape each portion into a ball. Allow each to rest 10 minutes covered with a polythene sheet. Flatten each ball and press into rectangles about 1in thick. Fold in half lengthwise and stretch dough gently until it is about three times the length of the baking pan. Fold the ends to the centre until they overlap, and press down firmly. Fold the dough in thirds lengthwise and seal by pressing down firmly. Roll the dough lightly with your hands and place in greased pans with seam side underneath. Each loaf should half-fill an $8\frac{1}{2} \times 4\frac{1}{2} \times 2\frac{1}{2}$in pan. Brush the tops of the loaves lightly with melted fat.

Set the pans in a warm place (80°F to 85°F) to rise (about 55 minutes). When the dough is doubled, it is ready to bake at 375°F (moderate oven) for 45 to 55 minutes. YIELD: 2 loaves.

Basic Sweet Rolls

Active dry yeast *or*	2 packages
Compressed yeast	2 cakes
Warm water (105–15°F)	$\frac{1}{4}$ cup
Milk	1 cup
Salt	2 teaspoons
Sugar	$\frac{1}{2}$ cup
Oil *or* soft shortening	$\frac{1}{4}$ cup
Sifted all-purpose flour	5 cups
Eggs	2
Grated lemon rind *or*	1 teaspoon
Lemon juice	$\frac{1}{2}$ teaspoon

Dissolve the yeast in lukewarm water. Scald the milk and

add sugar, salt and oil or shortening. Cool to lukewarm. Add enough flour to make a thick batter. Beat until smooth. Add dissolved or reconstituted yeast, eggs and lemon rind or juice. Beat well. Add the remaining flour—enough to make a soft but not sticky dough. Turn on to a lightly floured board or pastry cloth and knead until smooth and satiny. Place in a greased bowl, cover, and let rise in a warm place (80°F to 85°F) until doubled (about 90 minutes). When it is light, punch it down. Let rest 10 minutes. Divide into 1oz pieces and shape it into rolls. Place on greased baking sheets. Leave to rise until they have doubled (about 45 minutes). Bake at 350°F (moderate oven) for 20 to 30 minutes. YIELD: about 3½ dozen small rolls.

Yeast Rolls

Active dry yeast *or*	1 package
Compressed yeast	1 cake
Warm water (105–15°F)	¼ cup
Sugar	¼ cup
Butter *or* margarine	¼ cup
Salt	1 teaspoon
Scalded milk	1 cup
Eggs, beaten	1
Sifted flour	4 cups

Dissolve yeast in water. Add ½ teaspoon sugar. Add rest of sugar, fat and salt to hot milk. Stir until sugar is dissolved. Cool, then add egg. Stir in dissolved or reconstituted yeast. Stir flour into liquid ingredients until well mixed. If using an electric mixer, mix flour into the liquids at low speed, scraping dough from the beater occasionally, or use dough hook; then continue beating until dough has pulled cleanly away from sides of bowl several times. Turn dough out on to a lightly floured board. If it was mixed by hand, knead it quickly until smooth and elastic. Do not knead the dough if it was machine mixed.

Form dough into a smooth ball, place it in a greased bowl,

and turn it over once or twice to grease the surface. Cover and let rise in warm place (80°F to 85°F) until double in bulk—about 1 hour. Turn dough out on to board, knead well. Divide into 2oz pieces and shape into rolls as desired. Place in a greased pan or on a baking sheet. Cover with waxed paper or oiled polythene sheet and let rise in a warm place until double in bulk. Bake at 400°F (hot oven) for 15 to 20 minutes. YIELD: approx 14 rolls.

French Bread

Active dry yeast *or*	2 packages
Compressed yeast	2 cakes
Warm water	
(105–15°F)	½ cup
Sugar	2 teaspoons
Shortening	2 tablespoons
Salt	2 teaspoons
Sugar	2 tablespoons
Boiling water	2 cups
Sifted flour	8¾ cups

Combine yeast, warm water and 2 teaspoons sugar. If using dried yeast, allow to stand for 10 minutes. Add shortening, salt and 2 tablespoons sugar to the boiling water. Cool to lukewarm; add to yeast mixture. Stir in the flour, using just enough to make a dough that can be handled. Turn dough out on to a lightly floured board and knead until it is smooth and elastic. Form into a smooth ball, place in a greased bowl, and turn dough to grease the top. Cover and let rise in a warm place (80°F to 85°F) until double in size. Punch the dough down and divide it into two portions. Roll each portion into a 12 × 15in rectangle. Roll each rectangle up tightly as for jelly roll. Seal the edges well. Place loaves on a greased baking sheet, cover and let rise in a warm place until double in size. Using scissors, cut slits in each loaf every 2½in. Brush the loaves with a mixture of slightly beaten egg white and 1 tablespoon water. Bake at 400°F (hot oven) for about 25 minutes. YIELD: 2 large loaves.

Simple Yeast Bread

Warm water (105–15°F)	2½ cups
Active dry yeast *or*	2 packages
Compressed yeast	2 cakes
Instant non-fat dry milk	½ cup
Sugar	2 tablespoons
Salt	1 tablespoon
Cooking oil	⅓ cup
Sifted all-purpose flour	7–7½ cups

Measure water into large mixing bowl. Stir in 1 teaspoon of the sugar. Sprinkle yeast over water. Add dry milk, sugar, salt, oil and about 3¼ cups flour. Blend well. Beat 3 minutes at medium speed of mixer. By hand, gradually add remaining flour to form a very stiff dough. Toss dough on floured surface until no longer sticky. Knead until smooth, 1 to 2 minutes. Divide in half. Using a rolling pin, shape dough into a 12 × 6in rectangle. Roll up tightly, starting with 6in side. Seal edges and ends. Place, seam-side down, in well-greased 8½ × 4½in pans. Cover. Let rise in warm place until doubled in size, about 1 hour. Bake at pre-heated 375°F (moderate oven) for 35 to 45 minutes. Remove from pans immediately. Cool on wire rack. YIELD: 2 loaves.

Oatmeal Bread Deluxe

Salt	2 teaspoons
Boiling water	2 cups
Quick-cooking rolled oats	2 cups
Butter	2 tablespoons
Active dry yeast *or*	1 package
Compressed yeast	1 cake
Warm water	¾ cup

Dark brown sugar	⅓ cup firmly packed
Instant non-fat dry milk	1 cup
Sifted all-purpose flour	3½–4 cups
Butter, melted	

In a 2 quart saucepan, add salt to boiling water; stir in rolled oats. Remove from heat. Add butter and stir until melted. Cool to lukewarm. In a large mixing bowl sprinkle or crumble yeast over warm water in which 1 teaspoon of the sugar has been dissolved and stir until dissolved. Add brown sugar. Blend in oatmeal mixture. Stir in non-fat dry milk. Gradually stir in enough flour to make a soft dough. Place in buttered bowl, brush with melted butter, cover and allow to stand in warm place until doubled (1 to 1½ hours). On lightly floured surface, knead until smooth. Divide in half; shape each half into a loaf; place in 2 buttered loaf pans, 8½ × 4 × 2½in size. Brush with melted butter. Cover and allow to stand in warm place until doubled in size. Bake at preheated 375°F (moderate oven) for 35 to 40 minutes. Turn out on to wire rack to cool. YIELD: 2 loaves.

Sally Lunn Bread

Butter	½ cup (1 stick)
Sugar	⅓ cup
Eggs	2
Active dry yeast *or*	1 package
Compressed yeast	1 cake
Warm milk (105–15°F)	⅓ cup
Milk	⅔ cup
Sifted all-purpose flour	4 cups
Salt	1 teaspoon

In a mixing bowl, cream butter; add sugar and eggs and beat

until light and fluffy. Dissolve yeast in warm milk; add remaining milk. Sift together flour and salt; add to creamed mixture alternately with milk mixture, beginning and ending with dry ingredients. Cover and allow to stand in warm place until doubled in bulk (1½ hours). Punch down and turn into buttered ring mould, 6 cup (2½ pint) capacity; cover and allow to stand in warm place until doubled (30 minutes). Bake at preheated 350°F (moderate oven) for 25 to 30 minutes. Turn out immediately on to wire rack and cool, right side up. YIELD: 1 loaf.

Cherry Whirligig Rolls

Warm water	1 cup
Active dry yeast *or*	1 package
Compressed yeast	1 cake
Honey	¼ cup
Salt	1 teaspoon
Eggs	1
Soft butter	¼ cup
Maraschino cherries, drained and chopped	¼ cup
Sifted all-purpose flour	3½–4 cups
Filling:	
Flour	¼ cup
Honey	¼ cup
Butter	¼ cup
Maraschino cherry juice—sufficient to moisten	

Prepare filling by mixing flour, honey and butter with sufficient maraschino cherry juice to moisten.

Measure warm water in large mixing bowl. Sprinkle or crumble in yeast. Stir in honey, salt, egg, butter, blend well, then add cherries and slowly blend in flour. Grease fingers before kneading on lightly floured board until smooth and elastic; about 5 minutes. Place in greased bowl, turning to bring greased side up; cover—let rise in warm place until doubled in size, 1½ to 2 hours. Punch down, turn and let rise again until almost doubled in size, 30 to 40 minutes. Roll out on lightly floured board into rectangle 18 × 9in. Spread surface with filling. Roll up tightly. Seal well, cut into 18 slices. Put each slice in a greased muffin pan, cut side up. Cover and let rise in warm place, until doubled in size, 35 to 40 minutes. Bake at 375°F (moderate oven) for 20 to 25 minutes. Serve warm with hot beverage. YIELD: 18 rolls.

Honey Rye Bread

Honey	¼ cup
Salt	1 tablespoon
Shortening *or* oil	2 tablespoons
Caraway seeds (optional)	1 tablespoon
Milk, scalded	1½ cups
Active dry yeast *or*	2 packages
Compressed yeast	2 cakes
Water	1 cup
Light rye flour	3 cups
Sifted all-purpose flour	2½ cups
Butter, melted	

Add honey, salt, shortening and caraway seeds to milk; cool to lukewarm. Soften dry yeast in warm (110°F) water; or compressed yeast in lukewarm (85°F) water. Combine yeast with milk mixture; add rye flour and 1 cup all-purpose flour. Beat thoroughly. Add remaining flour to make stiff dough. Turn dough out on floured board, let rest 10 minutes. Oil fingers before kneading on lightly floured board until smooth and elastic. Place dough in well-greased bowl, turn once to bring greased side up. Cover and set in warm place (80°F to 85°F) to rise until doubled in bulk, about 40 minutes.

Without punching down, turn out on lightly floured board; divide into 2 equal parts. Shape into loaves. Place in 2 greased

9 × 5 × 3in pans. Cover and let rise until doubled in bulk, about 30 minutes. Bake at 350°F (moderate oven) for about 50 minutes. Turn out of pans on to cooling rack. Brush tops with melted butter. YIELD: 2 loaves.

TIP: For a chewy crust, lightly brush tops of loaves with warm water after 20 minutes of baking, repeat 2 or 3 times at 10 minute intervals.

Savory Cheese Bread

Milk	1 cup
Honey	¼ cup
Salt	1 tablespoon
Active dry yeast *or*	2 packages
Compressed yeast	2 cakes
Warm water	½ cup
Cheddar cheese, grated	1 cup
Dry mustard	1 teaspoon
Cayenne pepper	⅛ teaspoon
Sifted all-purpose flour	4½–5 cups

In a small saucepan, heat milk just until bubbles form around edge of pan. Remove from heat. Add honey and salt, stirring until dissolved. Let cool to lukewarm. Sprinkle or crumble yeast over warm water in large bowl, stirring until dissolved. Stir in milk mixture, cheese, mustard, cayenne pepper and 2 cups flour. Beat with wooden spoon until smooth, about 2 minutes. Gradually add remaining flour; mix in last of it by hand until dough leaves sides of the bowl. Turn dough on to lightly floured board. Oil fingers before kneading until smooth, about 10 minutes. Place in lightly greased large bowl, turn once to bring greased side up and cover. Let rise in warm place (85°F) until double in size, about 2 hours. Punch down dough, turn on to lightly floured board, shape into loaf. Place in greased 9 × 5 × 3in loaf pan. Cover loaf, let rise again until double, about

1 hour. Bake at 400°F (hot oven) for 30 to 35 minutes. Cover with aluminium foil last 10 to 15 minutes of baking. YIELD: 1 loaf.

Light and Tender Refrigerator Rolls

Warm water	1¾ cups
Mild flavored honey	½ cup
Active dry yeast *or*	2 packages
Compressed yeast	2 cakes
Egg, unbeaten	1
Butter *or* margarine, soft	¼ cup
Sifted all-purpose flour	6 cups
Salt	1 tablespoon

Mix together in large bowl warm water and honey. Blend in yeast. Beat in egg, soft butter, 3 cups flour and salt. Beat about 2 minutes or until smooth. Gradually add 1 cup of flour, beating hard. Using hands, work in balance of flour until dough is smooth and elastic. Grease top of dough. Cover with foil or polythene. Let rise in refrigerator at least 2 hours or until double in bulk. Punch down, refrigerate. Store in refrigerator 1 to 3 days, punching down once a day. Remove all or part of dough from refrigerator, shape into rolls. Cover; let rise in warm place (85°F) until double in bulk (about 1 hour). Heat oven to 400°F (hot oven). Brush rolls lightly with melted butter or margarine. Bake 12 to 15 minutes or until golden brown. YIELD: About 36 rolls.

Honey Wheat Bread

Milk	2 cups
Honey	⅓ cup
Salt	1 tablespoon
Shortening *or* oil	¼ cup
Active dry yeast *or*	2 packages
Compressed yeast	2 cakes

| Warm water | $\frac{1}{4}$ cup |
| Unsifted whole wheat flour | 5–7 cups |

Warm milk. Add honey, salt and shortening. Blend yeast with water. Add to milk mixture. Stir until smooth. Add flour in three parts, beating well after each addition until mixture is of stiff dough consistency. Turn on to lightly floured board or cloth. Grease fingers and knead until smooth and elastic (8 to 10 minutes). Place in greased bowl, turning to grease top. Cover, let rise in warm place (80°F to 85°F) until doubled in bulk (about 50 minutes). Without punching down, turn out on lightly floured board. Divide into two equal parts. Shape into loaves. Place in two greased 9 × 5 × 3in pans. Cover, let rise in warm place until doubled in bulk (about 50 minutes). Heat oven to 350°F (moderate oven). Bake 40 minutes or until done. Remove from pans, brush tops with melted butter and cool on wire rack. YIELD: 2 loaves.

Italian Style White Bread

Active dry yeast *or*	2 packages
Compressed yeast	2 cakes
Warm water	2$\frac{1}{2}$ cups
Honey	2 tablespoons
Salt	1 tablespoon
Melted shortening *or* salad oil	2 tablespoons
Unsifted all-purpose flour	7–8 cups

Sprinkle yeast over lukewarm water in large mixing bowl. Add honey. Let stand 5 minutes or until frothy. Mix until yeast is dissolved. Add salt, melted shortening and 3 cups of flour. Mix thoroughly with electric mixer or beat briskly. Mix in 3 more cups of flour. Sprinkle 1 cup flour on board. Turn out dough on to board. Knead until smooth (about 5 minutes). Add more flour if necessary. Place dough in greased bowl. Turn to grease top. Cover

and let rise in warm place until double in bulk (about 1½ hours).
Punch dough down and divide in half. To shape: roll half of
dough on floured board into a circle about 10in in diameter.
Grasp one edge and roll tightly similar to a jelly roll. Place on
baking sheet sprinkled with cornmeal. Tuck ends under. Repeat
operation for second loaf. Let loaves rise again until doubled in
bulk (about 1 hour). Heat oven to 375°F (moderate oven). Bake
about 30 minutes. YIELD: 2 loaves.

Rose Rolls

Unsifted flour	3¾–4¼ cups
Sugar	½ cup
Salt	2 teaspoons
Active dry yeast *or*	2 packages
Compressed yeast	2 cakes
Milk	¾ cup
Water	½ cup
Margarine	½ cup (1 stick)
Egg (at room temperature)	1
Cherry pie filling	1 can (1lb 6oz)
Confectioners' sugar frosting	

In a large bowl, thoroughly mix 1 cup flour, sugar, salt and
undissolved yeast. Combine milk, water and margarine in a
saucepan. Heat over low heat until liquids are very warm (120°F
to 130°F). Margarine does not need to melt. Gradually add to
dry ingredients and beat 2 minutes at medium speed of electric
mixer, scraping bowl occasionally. Add egg and ½ cup flour.
Beat at high speed 2 minutes, scraping bowl occasionally. Add
enough additional flour to make a stiff batter. Cover bowl tightly
with aluminium foil. Chill 2 hours (or overnight). Turn dough on
to lightly floured board; divide into 18 equal pieces. Gently roll
each piece to a rope, 15in long. Hold one end of each rope in
place and wind dough around loosely to form coil; tuck end
firmly underneath. Place on greased baking sheets about 2in

apart. Cover: let rise in warm place, free from draught, until doubled in bulk, about 1 hour. Make indentations about 1in wide in centre of each coil, pressing to bottom; fill with cherry pie filling. Bake at 400°F (hot oven) for 12 to 15 minutes or until done. Remove from baking sheets and cool on wire racks. When cool, drizzle with confectioners' sugar frosting. YIELD: 18 rolls.

Sixty-Minute Rolls

Unsifted flour	3½–4½ cups
Sugar	3 tablespoons
Salt	1 teaspoon
Active dry yeast *or*	2 packages
Compressed yeast	2 cakes
Milk	1 cup
Water	½ cup
Margarine	¼ cup

In a large bowl, thoroughly mix 1½ cups or ⅓ of the flour, sugar, salt and undissolved yeast. Combine milk, water and margarine in a saucepan. Heat over low heat until liquids are very warm (120°F to 130°F). Margarine does not need to melt. Gradually add to dry ingredients and beat 2 minutes at medium speed of electric mixer, scraping bowl occasionally. Add ½ cup flour. Beat at high speed, 2 minutes, scraping bowl occasionally. Stir in enough of the additional flour to make a soft dough. Turn out on to lightly floured board; knead until smooth and elastic, about 5 minutes. Place in greased bowl, turning to grease top. Cover; place bowl in pan of water at about 98°F. Let rise 15 minutes. Turn dough out on to floured board. Divide in half and shape as Curlicues or Lucky Clovers (below). Cover; let rise in warm place (about 90°F), 15 minutes. Bake at 425°F (hot oven) about 12 minutes or until done. Remove from baking sheets and cool on wire racks. YIELD: 24 rolls.

VARIATIONS: *Curlicues:* Roll out each half to a 12 × 9in rectangle. Cut into 12 equal strips about 1in wide. Hold one end of strip firmly and wind closely to form coil. Tuck end firmly underneath. Place on greased baking sheets about 2in apart.

Lucky Clovers: Form each half into a 12in roll. Cut into 12 equal pieces. Form into balls; place in greased muffin pans 2¾ × 1¼in. With scissors, cut each ball in half, then into quarters, cutting through almost to bottom of rolls.

Middle Eastern Bread

Unsifted flour	5–6 cups
Sugar	1 tablespoon
Salt	2 teaspoons
Active dry yeast *or*	1 package
Compressed yeast	1 cake
Warm water	2 cups

In a large bowl, thoroughly mix 2 cups or ⅓ of flour, sugar, salt and undissolved active dry yeast. Gradually add water to dry ingredients and beat 2 minutes at medium speed of electric mixer, scraping bowl occasionally. Add ¾ cup flour. Beat at high speed 2 minutes. Add ¾ cup flour. Beat at high speed 2 minutes, scraping bowl occasionally. Stir in enough of the additional flour to make a soft dough. Turn out on to lightly floured board; knead until smooth and elastic, about 8 to 10 minutes. Place in a greased bowl, turning to grease top. Cover; let rise in warm place until doubled in bulk, about 1 hour. Punch dough down; turn out on to lightly floured board. Cover; let rest 30 minutes. Divide dough into 6 equal pieces; shape each into a ball. On a lightly floured board, roll each ball into an 8in circle; place on a lightly floured baking sheet. Slide the circle directly on to the floor of a very hot oven, 450°F, or into a preheated iron skillet placed on the lowest rack of a very hot oven, 450°F. Bake about 5 minutes or until done. (Tops will not be brown.) Lightly brown tops of bread by placing under hot broiler (450°F) 3in from source of heat for about 1 minute or until browned. YIELD: 6 loaves.

Sweet Yeast Raised Bread

Cornmeal	¾ cup
Water	2 cups
Salt	2 teaspoons
Light molasses	½ cup
Butter *or* margarine	3 tablespoons
Active dry yeast *or*	1 package
Compressed yeast	1 cake
Warm water	¼ cup
Sifted all-purpose flour	6 cups

Combine cornmeal, water and salt in saucepan. Bring to a boil, stirring constantly. Remove from heat; add molasses and butter. Cool. Dissolve yeast in lukewarm water. Add 1 cup flour to cornmeal mixture. Stir in dissolved or reconstituted yeast. Stir in enough of the additional flour to make a soft dough. Turn out on lightly floured board; knead until smooth and satiny, about 5 minutes. Round dough into ball; place in greased bowl; brush lightly with melted shortening. Cover and let rise until double in size, about 1½ hours. Punch dough down. Divide in half; shape each half to form a round loaf. Place in two greased 8 or 9in (round) baking pans. Brush with melted shortening. Cover; let rise until nearly double in size, about 1 hour. Bake in preheated moderate oven 375°F for 50 to 60 minutes. YIELD: 2 loaves.

Quick Wheatmeal Rolls

Water	1¼ cups
Sugar	2 teaspoons
Active dry yeast *or*	1 package
Compressed yeast	1 cake
Sifted all-purpose flour	2 cups
Whole wheat flour	1¾ cups
Salt	2 teaspoons
Shortening	1 tablespoon
Cracked wheat or crushed cornflakes for sprinkling on top	

Measure water into a bowl. Stir in 1 teaspoon of sugar. Sprinkle or crumble yeast over water and stir to dissolve. Place all-purpose flour and whole wheat flour in a mixing bowl with salt and 1 teaspoon sugar. Rub in shortening. Add the dissolved or reconstituted yeast and mix to form a soft dough. Turn dough out on to a lightly floured board and knead until no longer sticky, about 2 minutes. Divide into 12 equal pieces and roll into rounds or flatten the dough to $\frac{1}{2}$in thick on a floured board and cut into rounds with a 2in cutter. Place on a greased baking sheet 2in. apart. Brush the tops with water and sprinkle with cracked wheat or crushed cornflakes. Cover, let rise in a warm place until doubled in bulk, about 1 hour. Bake near top of hot oven, 450°F for 15 to 20 minutes or until done. Remove from baking sheet and cool on wire rack. YIELD: 12 rolls.

Raised Cornmeal Rolls

Unsifted flour	$6\frac{1}{2}$–$7\frac{1}{2}$ cups
Yellow cornmeal	$1\frac{1}{2}$ cups
Sugar	$\frac{1}{2}$ cup
Salt	1 tablespoon
Active dry yeast *or*	2 packages
Compressed yeast	2 cakes
Milk	$1\frac{1}{2}$ cups
Water	$\frac{3}{4}$ cup
Margarine	$\frac{1}{2}$ cup
Eggs	2
Margarine melted for brushing rolls	

In a large bowl, thoroughly mix $1\frac{1}{2}$ cups or $\frac{1}{4}$ of the flour, cornmeal, sugar, salt and undissolved yeast. Combine milk, water and margarine in a saucepan. Heat over low heat until liquids are very warm (120°F to 130°F). Margarine does not need to melt. Gradually add to dry ingredients and beat 2 minutes at medium speed of electric mixer, scraping bowl occasionally. Add eggs and $\frac{1}{2}$ cup flour. Beat at high speed 2 minutes, scraping bowl occasionally. Stir in enough additional flour to make a stiff dough. Turn out on to lightly floured board; knead until smooth and elastic, about 8 to 10 minutes. Place in greased bowl, turning to grease top. Cover; let rise in warm place, until doubled in bulk, about 1 hour. Punch dough down; divide into 3 equal pieces. Proceed according to directions below for desired shape.

Muffin Rolls: Divide each piece of dough into 12 equal pieces. Form each piece into a smooth ball; place in greased muffin pans, 2¾ × 1¼in.

Pan Rolls: Divide each piece of dough into 9 equal pieces. Form each piece into a smooth ball; place 9 balls in each of 3 well-greased 8in square baking pans.

Brush rolls with melted margarine. Cover; let rise in warm place, free from draught, until doubled in bulk, about 1 hour. Bake at 375°F (moderate oven) 15 minutes for muffin rolls, 25 minutes for pan rolls, or until done. Remove from pans and cool on wire racks. Serve warm. YIELD: 27 to 36 rolls.

Potato Bread

Unsifted flour	4 cups
Sugar	2 teaspoons
Warm water	½ cup
Milk	½ cup
Active dry yeast *or*	1 package
Compressed yeast	1 cake
Boiled, mashed potatoes	1 cup
Melted shortening *or* oil	2 tablespoons
Salt	2 teaspoons

In a large mixing bowl, thoroughly mix 1 cup flour and the sugar, warm water, milk and dry or compressed yeast. Allow to stand in a warm place until frothy, about 20 minutes. Mix the potatoes, melted shortening or oil and salt into the batter and add enough of the remaining flour to make a stiff dough. Turn out on to a lightly floured board, knead until smooth and elastic, about 10 minutes. Place in greased bowl, turning once to grease top. Cover, let rise in warm place until doubled in bulk, about 1 hour. Punch dough down. Turn out on to a lightly floured board. Divide into 2 and knead each piece to form a smooth ball. Place on greased baking sheet. Press dough to flatten into a 7in circle. Cover; let rise in warm place until double in size, about 50 minutes. Bake at 400°F (hot oven) for about 25 minutes. The crust should be deep brown in color. Remove from baking sheet and cool on wire rack. YIELD: 2 loaves.

Onion Rolls

	1 cup
Sugar	2 tablespoons
Salt	2 teaspoons
Margarine	3 tablespoons
Warm water	1½ cups
Active dry yeast *or*	1 package
Compressed yeast	1 cake
Instant minced onion*	2 tablespoons
Unsifted flour	5–6 cups
Cornmeal for sprinkling baking sheets	
Egg white, slightly beaten	1
Cold water	1 tablespoon

Scald milk; stir in sugar, salt and margarine. Cool to luke-warm. Measure warm water into large warm bowl. Sprinkle or crumble in yeast. Stir until dissolved. Leave to stand for 10 minutes until frothy. Add warm milk mixture, onion and 3 cups or half the flour. Beat until smooth. Add enough of the additional flour to make a stiff dough. Turn out on to lightly floured board; knead until smooth and elastic, about 8 to 10 minutes. Place in greased bowl, turning to grease top. Cover; let rise in warm place, until doubled in bulk, about 1 hour. Punch dough down, divide into 14 equal pieces. Shape pieces of dough into round balls. Place about 3in apart on greased baking sheets, sprinkled with cornmeal. Cover; let rise in warm place, free from draught, until doubled in bulk, about 1 hour. Slit tops of rolls with sharp knife or razor in criss-cross fashion. Bake at 400°F (hot oven) for 20 minutes. Brush rolls with combined egg white and cold water. Bake for further 4 to 5 minutes or until done. Remove from baking sheets and cool on wire racks. YIELD: 14 rolls.

* 1 tablespoon instant minced onion is equivalent to 3 tablespoons finely chopped fresh onions.

Prairie Crescent Rolls

Active dry yeast *or*	1 package
Compressed yeast	1 cake
Warm water	$\frac{2}{3}$ cup
Sugar	2 tablespoons
Shortening	2 tablespoons
All-purpose butter- milk biscuit mix*	2$\frac{1}{2}$ cups
Soft butter *or* margarine for brushing baked rolls	

Dissolve yeast in warm water. Allow to stand for 10 minutes. Stir in sugar, shortening and baking mix; beat vigorously. Turn dough on to floured board. Knead until smooth, about 20 times. Roll dough into 12in circle. Cut into 16 wedges. Roll up, beginning at rounded edge. Place rolls with points underneath on lightly greased baking sheet. Cover and let rise in warm place until double, about 30 minutes. Heat oven to 400°F (hot oven). Bake 10 to 15 minutes or until golden brown. While hot, brush with butter. YIELD: 16 rolls.

* See p 20 for alternative to all-purpose buttermilk biscuit mix.

11

Lunch-Brunch Bread

Just a few simple additions, and bread can become a gourmet special treat. Here are some of the most flavorful ways in which you can transform bread into a culinary creation. Enjoy these 'super' breads for lunch or brunch or with a hot beverage and enter a world of exotic taste thrill.

Brunch Bran Date Muffins

Bran Flakes	1 cup
Milk	1 cup
Butter *or* margarine, softened	2 tablespoons
Molasses *or* granulated sugar	¼ cup
Eggs, well beaten	1
Sifted, all-purpose flour	1 cup
Baking powder	1 tablespoon
Salt	½ teaspoon
Dates, chopped	½ cup

In medium bowl, soak bran in milk for 5 minutes. Set aside. Cream together butter and molasses or sugar; then add egg. Blend but do not beat. Stir into bran. Sift together flour, baking powder and salt. Add with chopped dates to bran mixture; stir until just blended. Fill 12 muffin cups ⅔ full. Bake in a preheated hot oven, 400°F for 20 to 25 minutes or until done. YIELD: About 12 medium muffins.

Southern Rice Bites

Water	$\frac{2}{3}$ cup
Salt	$\frac{1}{4}$ teaspoon
Butter	1 tablespoon
Pre-cooked rice	$\frac{2}{3}$ cup
Eggs, well beaten	1
Milk	$\frac{1}{3}$ cup
Grated onion	2 teaspoons
Unsifted all-purpose flour	$\frac{1}{4}$ cup
Baking powder	$1\frac{1}{2}$ teaspoons
Sugar	1 teaspoon
Salt	$\frac{1}{4}$ teaspoon
Pepper	$\frac{1}{8}$ teaspoon

Bring water, $\frac{1}{4}$ teaspoon salt and butter to a boil. Stir in rice. Cover, remove from heat, and let stand 5 minutes. Meanwhile, combine egg, milk and onion; then mix into rice. Combine remaining ingredients, add to rice mixture and mix only enough to dampen flour. Drop by tablespoonfuls on to hot well-greased griddle; brown lightly on both sides. Serve hot with currant jelly or maple syrup. YIELD: Makes 10 to 12 festive breads or 5 to 6 servings.

VARIATION: *Cheese Rice Bites:* Prepare as above, adding $\frac{1}{2}$ cup diced Cheddar cheese with the egg mixture.

Easy Pizza

Sifted all-purpose flour	2 cups
Baking powder	3 teaspoons
Salt	1 teaspoon
Olive oil	4 tablespoons
Milk	$\frac{1}{3}$ cup
Tomato paste	1 can (8oz)
Onion, chopped	2 tablespoons

Dried marjoram	1 tablespoon
Anchovy fillets	1 can (2oz)
Green olives,	
chopped	½ cup
Hard cheese, grated	½ cup

Sift together flour, baking powder and salt. Stir in olive oil and milk. Add a little more milk, if necessary, to form a stiff dough. Turn out on lightly floured board and knead lightly for a minute or two. Roll out ½in thick and place in a round cake pan, allowing edges to curve slightly up sides of pan. Spread with tomato paste mixed with onion. Sprinkle with marjoram; lay on anchovy fillets. Bake at 450°F (very hot oven) for 18 to 20 minutes. Just before removing from oven, sprinkle on chopped olives and cheese to melt. YIELD: Very large pizza, serving 4 or 6.

Lemony Bread Pudding

Milk	4 cups
Mild flavored honey	⅔ cup
Dry bread cubes,	4 cups (about
½in size	10 slices)
Eggs	6
Salt	½ teaspoon
Grated lemon rind	2 teaspoons
Gesh lemon juice	2 tablespoons
Nutmeg (optional) for sprinkling top	

Warm milk and honey together. Prepare bread cubes, removing crust. Place in 2 quart buttered casserole. Beat eggs slightly with salt. Add to bread cubes with honey mixture, lemon rind and juice. Sprinkle top with nutmeg. Heat oven to 300°F (slow oven). Bake 50 to 60 minutes or until custard is set near center. May be served warm or cold. YIELD: 8 servings.

Almond Yeast Buns

Roasted almonds, diced	½ cup
Light or dark raisins	½ cup
Chopped citron	¼ cup
Hot roll mix*	1 package (14½oz)
Sugar	¼ cup
Cinnamon	½ teaspoon
Nutmeg	½ teaspoon
Eggs, separated	1
Almond extract	Few drops
Candied cherries	6
Blanched almonds, halved, for garnish	

Chop almonds. Rinse and drain raisins; add citron, roll mix sugar, spice and diced almonds. Mix well. Add liquid to yeast as directed on package, reducing liquid by 2 tablespoons. Beat egg yolk lightly and mix into yeast mixture with almond extract. Stir into dry mixture, blending thoroughly. Shape into 12 round buns and place on greased baking sheet. Cover; allow to stand in warm place until doubled in bulk, about 1 to 1½ hours. Brush tops with egg white beaten until foamy. Top each with a cherry half and several almond halves. Bake at 375°F (moderate oven) for about 25 minutes. Serve warm. YIELD: 12 (3in) rolls.

* See pp 20–1 for alternative to hot roll mix.

California Fruit Loaf

Butter, softened	¼ cup
Dark brown sugar	⅓ cup
Grated lemon rind	2 teaspoons
Grated orange rind	2 teaspoons
Eggs, unbeaten	1
Creamed cottage cheese	1 cup

Sifted flour	1½ cups
Baking powder	1½ teaspoons
Baking soda	½ teaspoon
Salt	1 teaspoon
Dried prunes, chopped	½ cup
Dried apricots, chopped	½ cup

Cream softened butter, sugar and rinds. Add egg; beat well. Stir in cheese. Sift flour, baking powder, baking soda and salt; add to first mixture along with fruits. Mix well. Mixture will be stiff. Pack in buttered loaf pan, 8½ × 4½ × 3in. Bake at 350°F (moderate oven) for about 1 hour. Cool. Wrap. Store in refrigerator. This loaf slices best after stored several hours. YIELD: 1 loaf.

Onion Flavoured Hush Puppies

Cornmeal	1 cup
Sifted all-purpose flour	⅓ cup
Salt	1 teaspoon
Baking powder	1 teaspoon
Baking soda	½ teaspoon
Onion, finely chopped	⅓ cup
Milk	¾ cup

Sift together cornmeal, flour, salt, baking powder, baking soda. Stir in onion. Add milk, mixing well. Drop batter by teaspoonfuls into hot, deep oil (375°F), frying only a few at a time. Fry until golden brown. Drain on absorbent paper. YIELD: About 18.

Tangerine Bread

Sifted flour	2 cups
Sugar	1 cup
Baking powder	2½ teaspoons
Salt	1 teaspoon

Baking soda	$\frac{1}{4}$ teaspoon
Tangerine peel, minced	3 tablespoons
Pecans *or* walnuts, chopped	$\frac{1}{2}$ cup
Eggs, well beaten	1
Tangerine juice	$\frac{1}{2}$ cup
Milk	$\frac{1}{2}$ cup
Butter *or* margarine, melted	$\frac{1}{4}$ cup

Sift together dry ingredients into large mixing bowl; stir in minced peel and nuts. Thoroughly combine remaining ingredients; add all at once to dry ingredients. Stir quickly until well blended. Pour into 9 × 5 × 3in loaf pan that has been well greased on the bottom. Bake at 325°F (slow oven) for 55 to 60 minutes or until done. Let stand 10 minutes before turning out on wire rack for complete cooling. This loaf cuts well and may be served as soon as it is cool. YIELD: 1 large loaf.

Pineapple Bread

Packaged baking mix*	$2\frac{1}{2}$ cups
Sugar	$\frac{1}{2}$ cup
Crushed pineapple, not drained	1 can ($8\frac{1}{4}$oz)
Eggs	1
Milk	$\frac{1}{4}$ cup
Nuts, chopped	$\frac{1}{2}$ cup

Preheat oven to 350°F (moderate oven). Now grease a loaf pan, 9 × 5in. Combine all ingredients except nuts. Beat vigorously with spoon for $\frac{1}{2}$ minute. Stir in nuts. Pour into prepared pan and bake 45 to 50 minutes. YIELD: 1 loaf. TIP: Have a Hawaiian Bread by using the same recipe, only substitute coarsely chopped macadamia nuts.

* See pp 19–20 for alternative to packaged baking mix.

Banana Nut Bread

Packaged baking mix*	2 cups
Sugar	1 cup
Shortening	¼ cup
Eggs	2
Bananas, crushed	1 cup (about 3 bananas)
Nuts, chopped	⅓ cup

Preheat oven to 350°F (moderate oven). Grease loaf pan, 9 × 5in. Combine all ingredients except nuts. Beat vigorously with spoon for ½ minute. Stir in nuts. Pour into prepared pan and bake about 50 minutes. YIELD: 1 loaf.

* See pp 19–20 for alternative to packaged baking mix.

Carrot Bread

Packaged baking mix*	2 cups
Sugar	¾ cup
Cinnamon	1 teaspoon
Carrots, grated	2 cups
Eggs	2
Shortening, melted	⅓ cup
Nuts, chopped	½ cup

Preheat oven to 350°F (moderate oven). Grease loaf pan, 9 × 5in. In a large bowl, blend all ingredients. Pour into prepared pan and bake 45 to 50 minutes. YIELD: 1 loaf.

* See pp 19–20 for alternative to packaged baking mix.

Treat Time Fruit Bread

Active dry yeast *or*	1 package
Compressed yeast	1 cake
Warm water (105-15°F)	½ cup

Eggs	1
Sugar	1 tablespoon
All-purpose butter-milk biscuit mix*	2½ cups
Mixed candied fruit	½ cup
Nuts, chopped	¼ cup

Dissolve yeast in warm water. Mix in egg, sugar and baking mix; beat vigorously. Stir in fruit and nuts. Drop dough by tablespoonfuls into greased square pan, 8 × 8 × 2in. Cover and let rise in warm place until double, about 1 hour. Heat oven to 400°F (hot oven). Bake 15 minutes or until golden brown. YIELD: Serves 9.

* See p 20 for alternative to all-purpose buttermilk biscuit mix.

Graham Date Bread

Sifted all-purpose flour	½ cup
Salt	½ teaspoon
Baking powder	1½ teaspoons
Graham cracker crumbs	1⅔ cups
Light brown sugar	½ cup firmly packed
Dates, chopped	8oz package
Walnuts *or* pecans, chopped	1 cup
Orange rind, grated	2 teaspoons
Eggs, well beaten	2
Orange juice	½ cup
Butter *or* margarine, melted	½ cup

Sift together first three ingredients. Add next five ingredients; mix well. Combine eggs, orange juice and butter. Stir into dry ingredients, mixing just until combined. Turn into a greased 8½ × 4½ × 2½in loaf pan. Bake in a preheated slow oven, 350°F for 60 to 65 minutes or until cake tester inserted in center comes out clean. Let cool, in pan, on wire rack 10 minutes. Turn out and cool completely. Store, aluminium foil-wrapped overnight, for easy slicing. YIELD: 1 large loaf.

12

Recipes for Allergics

Baking breads for family members allergic to wheat, eggs or milk calls for special recipes. The recipes in this chapter were developed for use without some or all of these basic ingredients. Those members of the family on a gluten-free diet must avoid recipes containing both wheat and rye flours. Every recipe has been tested for flavor, texture and appearance of the final product. Muffins made without eggs may crumble more readily than those made with eggs. Breads made with non-wheat flours may not be as light as those made with wheat flour. Also, muffins and biscuits may not have as rich a brown color when flours other than wheat are used. But the taste is delicious and should make up for any slight inconveniences. The ingredients are commonly available at most markets; if not, try the speciality food stores.

Rye Biscuits

(Without eggs or wheat)

Rye flour	1⅓ cups
Soybean flour	½ cup
Sugar	2 tablespoons
Baking powder	1 tablespoon
Salt	1 teaspoon
Shortening	¼ cup
Milk	¾ cup

Preheat oven to 450°F (very hot). Mix dry ingredients thoroughly. Mix or rub in shortening only until mixture is crumbly. Add milk gradually, and stir until a soft dough is formed. Place on floured surface and roll or pat to a thickness of about ½in. Cut into 2in rounds. Place on ungreased baking sheet. Bake 12 minutes or until very lightly browned. YIELD: 12 biscuits.

Orange Nut Bread

(Without eggs, milk or wheat)

Rolled oats, ground	2¼ cups
Baking powder	4 teaspoons
Baking soda	¼ teaspoon
Salt	¾ teaspoon
Sugar	¾ cup
Nuts, chopped	¾ cup
Cooking oil	2 tablespoons
Orange juice	¾ cup
Grated orange rind	1 tablespoon

Preheat oven to 350°F (moderate oven). Grease 9 × 5in loaf pan. Mix dry ingredients thoroughly. Add nuts, oil, orange juice and rind. Stir until dry ingredients are well moistened. Pour into pan. Bake 60 minutes or until firm to touch. To prevent the top of loaf from cracking, cover with aluminium foil during the first 20 minutes of baking. TIP: Grind rolled oats in a food chopper or liquidiser, using the fine cutting blade. YIELD: 1 loaf.

Cornmeal Muffins

(Without eggs, milk or wheat)

Cornmeal	1 cup
Rye flour	½ cup
Rice flour	⅓ cup
Baking powder	2 tablespoons
Salt	¾ teaspoon
Sugar	¼ cup
Water	1 cup
Shortening, melted	¼ cup

Preheat oven to 375°F (moderate oven). Grease 12 muffin pans. Mix dry ingredients thoroughly. Add water and shortening; mix well. Fill muffin pans about half full. Bake 30 minutes or until very lightly browned and firm to touch. YIELD: 12 small muffins.

Spoonbread
(Without wheat)

Milk	3 cups
Cornmeal	1 cup
Salt	1½ teaspoons
Butter *or* margarine	2 tablespoons
Egg yolks, beaten	4
Egg whites	4

Preheat oven to 400°F (hot oven). Grease 1½ quart casserole. Combine milk, cornmeal and salt. Cook over low heat, stirring constantly, until thickened. Add butter. Cool the mixture. Stir in egg yolks. Beat egg whites until stiff, but not dry. Fold into cornmeal mixture. Pour into casserole. Bake 35 to 40 minutes or until set. Serve hot. YIELD: 6 servings.

Rolled Oat Muffins
(Without eggs, milk or wheat)

Rolled oats, ground	1 cup
Rice flour	¾ cup
Baking powder	2 tablespoons
Salt	1 teaspoon
Cinnamon	1 teaspoon
Sugar	¼ cup
Raisins	½ cup
Water	1¼ cups
Oil	¼ cup

Preheat oven to 425°F (hot oven). Grease 12 muffin pans. Mix dry ingredients thoroughly. Add raisins, water and oil. Mix well. Fill muffin pans about ⅔ full. Bake 20 minutes or until lightly

browned. TIP: Grind rolled oats in a food chopper or liquidiser,
using the fine cutting blade. YIELD: 12 medium size muffins.

Rye Crackers

(Without eggs or wheat)

Rye flour	1¾ cups
Rice flour	1 cup
Salt	1½ teaspoons
Baking soda	1 teaspoon
Oil	½ cup
Buttermilk	1 cup

Preheat oven to 375°F (moderate oven). Mix dry ingredients
thoroughly. Mix in oil only until mixture is crumbly. Add buttermilk and mix well. Place dough on a well-floured surface. Roll
very thin. Cut into strips 3 × 1½in. Place with sides touching on
baking sheet. Bake 18 minutes or until lightly browned. YIELD:
About 75 crackers, 3 × 1½in in size.

Rye Muffins

(Without eggs, milk or wheat)

Rye flour	1¼ cups
Rice flour	½ cup
Baking powder	4 teaspoons
Salt	¾ teaspoon
Sugar	¼ cup
Water	1 cup
Oil	¼ cup

Preheat oven to 375°F (moderate oven). Mix dry ingredients
thoroughly. Add water and oil; mix well. Fill 12 greased muffin
pans about half full. Bake 25 minutes or until lightly browned.
YIELD: 12 small muffins.

Waffles

(Without wheat)

Rice flour	1½ cups
Baking powder	1 tablespoon
Salt	1 teaspoon
Milk	1½ cups
Egg yolks, beaten	2
Oil	3 tablespoons
Egg whites, stiffly beaten	2

Mix dry ingredients well. Beat in milk, egg yolks and oil. Fold in egg whites. Bake in hot waffle iron. YIELD: 16 waffles, 7in in diameter.

Fig Nut Breadless Pudding

(Without milk or wheat)

Eggs	2
Sugar	¾ cup
Rice flour	3 tablespoons
Baking powder	1 teaspoon
Salt	¼ teaspoon
Cinnamon	½ teaspoon
Dried figs, chopped	1 cup
Nuts, chopped	1 cup

Preheat oven to 300°F (slow oven). Grease an 8 x 8 x 2in baking pan. Beat eggs until thick and light in colour. Add sugar to eggs gradually, beating constantly. Mix dry ingredients. Stir into egg mixture. Add figs and nuts. Beat thoroughly. Pour into baking pan. Bake 40 minutes or until mixture is firm to touch. YIELD: Serves 6.

Fruit Bread

(Without eggs or milk)

Sifted all-purpose flour	1¾ cups
Double acting baking powder	2 teaspoons
Baking soda	¼ teaspoon
Salt	½ teaspoon
Oil	⅓ cup
Granulated sugar	⅔ cup
Bananas, mashed	1 cup (about 3 bananas)

Preheat oven to 350°F (moderate). Grease a 9 × 5 × 3in loaf pan. Sift together the flour, baking powder, baking soda and salt. Next, cream the oil and sugar. In an electric mixer at low speed, combine the dry ingredients with the creamed mixture and the bananas. Beat until just smooth. Turn into prepared pan. Bake 1 hour or until a cake tester, inserted in center, comes out clean. Cool in pan 10 minutes; remove. TIP: Cool overnight before slicing and serving the next day. YIELD: 1 large loaf or about 16 slices.

Simple Rye Bread

(Without eggs, milk or wheat)

Active dry yeast *or*	1 package
Compressed yeast	1 cake
Warm water (105–15°F)	¼ cup
Salt	2 teaspoons
Dark brown sugar	1 tablespoon
Water	1 cup
Rye flour	4 cups

Dissolve yeast in warm water. Combine with salt, sugar and remaining water. Stir in rye flour. Beat smooth. Turn out on to

a rye-floured board, then knead, using more rye flour to create
a firm, elastic dough. Place in greased bowl. Brush top with
salad oil. Cover; let rise in a warm place (about 85°F) until
double in bulk. Knead. Place in bowl again, cover and let rise
once more, about 1 hour. Shape into a loaf. Place in a greased
9 × 5 × 3in loaf pan. Cover with plastic or polythene film. Let
rise until double in bulk. Bake in 450°F (very hot) oven for 15
minutes. Reduce heat to 350°F (moderate) and bake 55 minutes
longer. YIELD: 1 loaf.

Rye Fruit Bread
(Without eggs, milk or wheat)

Active dry yeast *or*	1 package
Compressed yeast	1 cake
Warm water	1½ tablespoons
Granulated sugar	2½ teaspoons
Salt	1½ teaspoons
Cooking oil	1½ tablespoons
Bananas, mashed	1 cup (about 3 bananas)
Unsifted rye flour	3 cups

Dissolve yeast in water and set aside. Combine sugar, salt,
cooking oil and bananas. Add 1½ cups unsifted rye flour. Beat
until smooth. Stir in dissolved yeast, then slowly add 1¼ cups
unsifted rye flour and mix well. Turn out on to rye-floured board;
knead until smooth, about 8 minutes. Place dough in greased
bowl. Cover. Let rise in warm place (85°F to 95°F) until double
in bulk. Knead lightly about 2 minutes. Shape into a loaf; place
in lightly greased 9 × 5 × 3in loaf pan. Brush top with salad oil.
Cover with a plastic or polythene film; let rise again until double
in bulk, and bake in 425°F (hot) oven until crust begins to brown,
about 5 to 10 minutes. Reduce heat to 350°F and bake 35 to 40
minutes more. YIELD: 1 loaf.

Creative Corn Muffins

(Without gluten or wheat)

White or yellow cornmeal	1 cup
Rice flour	¾ cup
Double acting baking powder	4 teaspoons
Salt	½ teaspoon
Granulated sugar	¼ cup
Egg whites	1
Egg yolks	1
Butter *or* margarine, melted	¼ cup
Milk	1 cup

Preheat oven to 425°F (hot oven). Meanwhile, grease 12 medium muffin pan cups. In a medium bowl, stir together cornmeal, rice flour, baking powder, salt and sugar. Now beat 1 egg white until stiff, but not dry, until peaks form. To all dry ingredients, add 1 egg yolk, butter and milk; stir until just smooth. Now fold in beaten egg white. Divide batter among muffin cups (about ¼ cup each) and bake 25 minutes or until sides of muffins brown lightly and pull away from cups. Turn muffins out. Serve warm. YIELD: 12 muffins.

Exceptional Muffins

(Without milk or wheat)

Unsifted rye flour	1¼ cups
Yellow cornmeal	¾ cup
Granulated sugar	¼ cup
Double acting baking powder	4½ teaspoons
Salt	1 teaspoon
Water	⅔ cup
Salad oil	⅓ cup
Eggs	1

Preheat oven to 425°F (hot oven). Generously grease 18 medium muffin cups. Into a large bowl, sift together flour, cornmeal, sugar, baking powder and salt. Now, in a medium bowl, beat together water, salad oil and egg. Add to flour mixture; mix until dry ingredients are slightly dampened, but not smooth. Spoon batter into muffin cups, filling ⅓ to ½ full. Bake 25 to 30 minutes or until muffins separate from pans; promptly turn out of pans. YIELD: 18.

Quick 'n' Easy Rye Muffins
(Without eggs, milk or wheat)

Unsifted rye flour	1 cup
Double acting baking powder	2 teaspoons
Granulated sugar	2 tablespoons
Salt	¼ teaspoon
Water	½ cup
Salad oil	2 tablespoons

Preheat oven to 400°F (hot oven). Grease 6 medium muffin cups. Sift together flour, baking powder, sugar and salt. Stir in until just mixed, but still lumpy, water and salad oil. Mix until the consistency of batter. Divide batter among muffin cups. Bake 30 to 35 minutes or until muffins come away from edges of pan. YIELD: 6 muffins.

VARIATIONS: *Pineapple Muffins:* To basic recipe, reduce sugar to 1 tablespoon; stir 2 tablespoons drained, canned, crushed pineapple into dry ingredients; substitute ½ cup pineapple juice for water.

Cinnamon Raisin Muffins: To basic recipe, stir ½ teaspoon cinnamon and ½ cup raisins into dry ingredients.

Nut Muffins: To basic recipe, add ½ cup chopped nuts to dry ingredients.

Date Muffins: To basic recipe, add ¼ cup cut-up pitted dates to dry ingredients.

Peanut Butter Muffins: To basic recipe, cut ¼ cup peanut butter into dry ingredients until smooth consistency; omit salad oil.

Better Rye Biscuits

(Without eggs, milk or wheat)

Unsifted rye flour	1 cup
Double acting baking powder	1½ teaspoons
Salt	¼ teaspoon
Shortening	3 tablespoons
Water	3 tablespoons

Preheat oven to 450°F (very hot oven). Grease a baking sheet. Now sift together the flour, baking powder, salt. Cut or rub in shortening until mixture is like coarse cornmeal. Stir in water to form a thick, pliable dough. Turn on to lightly rye-floured board; roll about 1½in thick. Cut with 2in cutter. Place on greased baking sheet. Bake 12 to 15 minutes. YIELD: 6 biscuits.

Gluten-Free Bread

(Without eggs and gluten)

Active dry yeast *or*	1 package
Compressed yeast	1 cake
Sugar	1 teaspoon
Warm water	⅔ cup
Wheat starch (not flour)	1¾ cups
Casilan*	2 tablespoons
Salt	1 teaspoon
Warm milk	½ cup

Grease and line a small loaf pan. Grease the lining paper. Dissolve yeast and sugar in warm water. Mix wheat starch, Casilan, salt, and cut or rub in fat. Add dissolved yeast and warm (not hot) milk and beat thoroughly. Cover and allow to rise in a warm place for 20 minutes. Beat again thoroughly and turn into the prepared loaf pan. Cover with polythene sheet and allow to rise until ½in from top of tin. Bake on middle shelf of preheated oven, 450°F (very hot oven) for 10 minutes before turning out on to wire rack. YIELD: 1 loaf.

* Milk protein, obtainable from most druggists or special health food stores.

Pancakes Unique

(Without wheat or gluten)

Rice flour	1½ cups
Potato starch flour	2 tablespoons
Corn starch	3 tablespoons
Double acting baking powder	1½ teaspoons
Salt	½ teaspoon
Lemon juice	1 teaspoon
Apple sauce	1 cup
Butter *or* margarine, melted	3 tablespoons
Milk	1 cup
Egg yolks	2
Egg whites	2

Preheat a lightly greased griddle until a drop of water 'dances' on top. Meanwhile, in a medium bowl, stir together rice flour, potato starch flour, corn starch, baking powder and salt. Now add lemon juice, apple sauce, butter, milk and egg yolks. Mix only until dry ingredients are dampened. Meanwhile, in a small bowl, beat 2 egg whites until stiff peaks form; fold beaten egg whites into batter. Drop by ¼ cupfuls on to heated griddle. Gently spread each pancake with back of spoon into a circle about 4in in diameter. Cook until rim of each is full of broken bubbles and underside is brown. Turn and brown other side. YIELD: About 16.

Great Griddle Cakes

(Without gluten or wheat)

Rice flour	1 cup
Double acting baking powder	1½ teaspoons
Granulated sugar	3 tablespoons
Salt	½ teaspoon
Egg, lightly beaten	1
Milk	1 cup
Butter, melted	3 tablespoons

Preheat lightly greased griddle according to manufacturer's directions. Meanwhile, in a medium bowl stir together flour, baking powder, sugar and salt. Combine 1 lightly beaten egg, milk and butter and add to dry ingredients. Mix well. Drop batter, from a tablespoon, on to griddle. Cook on one side until full of bubbles. Turn and brown other side. YIELD: About 12.

Waffles Wonderama

(Without gluten or wheat)

Yellow cornmeal	½ cup
Potato starch flour	½ cup
Corn starch	2 tablespoons
Double acting baking powder	1½ teaspoons
Salt	¼ teaspoon
Granulated sugar	1 tablespoon
Eggs	1
Milk (or water)	½ cup
Butter or margarine, melted	3 tablespoons

Preheat waffle iron according to manufacturer's directions. Meanwhile, stir together cornmeal, potato starch flour, corn starch, baking powder, salt and sugar. Now beat egg until light and add milk and melted butter. Slowly mix into dry ingredients until smooth. Bake waffles according to manufacturer's directions. YIELD: 2 or 3 large waffles.

Great Gingerbread

(Without milk or wheat)

Shortening	$\frac{1}{3}$ cup
Granulated sugar	$\frac{1}{3}$ cup
Eggs, well-beaten	1
Molasses	$\frac{3}{4}$ cup
Sifted rye flour	$2\frac{1}{4}$ cups
Baking soda	$1\frac{1}{2}$ teaspoons
Cloves, ground	$\frac{1}{2}$ teaspoon
Cinnamon, ground	1 teaspoon
Ginger, ground	1 teaspoon
Salt	$\frac{1}{2}$ teaspoon
Hot water	$\frac{1}{4}$ cup

Preheat oven to 350°F (moderate). Meanwhile, grease and flour (with rye flour) a 9 × 9 × 2in loaf pan. Now cream the shortening with the sugar until fluffy. Beat in the egg and molasses. Next, sift the rye flour, baking soda, cloves, cinnamon, ginger and salt. Beat $\frac{1}{3}$ of the dry ingredients into the shortening mixture. Beat in the hot water. Repeat. Beat in remaining dry ingredients. Beat well. Turn into loaf pan. Bake 50 to 55 minutes or until bread comes away from edge of pan. YIELD: 1 loaf.

13

Spice and Herb Flavored Breads

The addition of one or more herbs or spices can put a startling new taste into most baked goods. Open a world of delicious good taste by using herbs in your baked goods. In most cases, a sprinkle of desired herbs or spices in almost any recipe will impart a flavor that is without comparison among other ingredients. Herbs and spices truly make the 'staff of life' a 'royal sceptre of good taste'.

Spice Flavored Apple Bread

Sifted all-purpose flour	3 cups
Baking soda	1½ teaspoons
Salt	1½ teaspoons
Cinnamon, ground	1½ teaspoons
Nutmeg, grated	¾ teaspoon
Allspice, ground	½ teaspoon
Cloves, ground	¼ teaspoon
Shortening	¾ cup
Light brown sugar	1⅛ cups, firmly packed
Eggs	3
Vanilla	1½ teaspoons
Raw apples, grated	1½ cups
Cider vinegar	3 tablespoons
Water	¾ cup less 3 tablespoons
Walnuts, chopped	¾ cup

Mix and sift flour, baking soda, salt and spices. Cream shortening and sugar. Add eggs 1 at a time, beating well after each addition. Add vanilla. Stir in flour mixture, alternating with grated apples and liquid. Stir in walnuts. Turn into greased loaf pan, $11\frac{1}{4} \times 4\frac{1}{2} \times 2\frac{1}{2}$in, or 2 small loaf pans. Bake at 350°F (moderate oven) for 75 minutes or until done. Cool on wire rack. YIELD: 2 small loaves.

Herb Parmesan Biscuits

Packaged biscuit mix*	2 cups
Sesame seeds	1 tablespoon
Leaf oregano	$\frac{1}{2}$ teaspoon
Allspice, ground	$\frac{1}{4}$ teaspoon
Butter	$\frac{1}{4}$ cup ($\frac{1}{2}$ stick)
Milk	$\frac{1}{2}$ cup
Eggs, beaten	1
Parmesan cheese, grated	$\frac{1}{2}$ cup

In a bowl, mix together biscuit mix, sesame seeds, oregano and allspice. Cut or rub in butter until mixture resembles coarse meal. Add milk, stirring with a fork to make a soft dough. On surface dusted with biscuit mix, knead dough about 10 times. Pat or roll $\frac{1}{2}$in thick. Cut with a floured 2in diameter cutter and place on baking sheet. Brush tops with egg; sprinkle with a generous teaspoonful of Parmesan cheese. Bake in preheated 450°F (very hot) oven for 10 minutes. YIELD: 12 biscuits.

* See pp 19–20 for alternative to packaged biscuit mix.

Herb Corn Muffins

Packaged corn muffin mix	2 cups
Eggs, unbeaten	1
Sour cream	$\frac{1}{3}$ cup
Thyme, ground	$\frac{1}{4}$ teaspoon

Salt	½ teaspoon
Celery seeds	½ teaspoon
Onion, grated	2 teaspoons

Combine all ingredients. Mix gently until well blended and dry ingredients are just moistened. Drop by spoonfuls into small, buttered muffin pans until ⅔ full. Bake according to package directions until done. YIELD: 12 small muffins.

Spice Flavored Rolls

Brown 'n' serve rolls	2 packages (24 rolls)
Butter *or* margarine	2 tablespoons
Light corn syrup	2 tablespoons
Light brown sugar	½ cup, firmly packed
Cinnamon, ground	1 teaspoon
Ginger, ground	1 teaspoon
Pecans, chopped	¼ cup

Bake rolls according to package directions. Melt butter and combine with remaining ingredients, except pecans. Stir until dissolved. Now add pecans and pour over the tops of the rolls during last 5 minutes of baking. Serve warm. YIELD: 24 rolls.

Caraway Seed Party Rolls

Hot roll mix*	1 package
Caraway seeds	¼ cup
Egg whites	1
Caraway seeds	2 tablespoons

Prepare hot roll mix according to directions on package, add ¼ cup caraway seeds to dry mix. Let rise according to directions. Punch down and work dough on a lightly floured board, kneading about 1 minute. Pinch off pieces of dough and roll between palms to 5in lengths. Shape into bow-knots. Place on lightly greased baking sheets. Beat 1 egg until foamy and brush over top of rolls. Sprinkle with 2 tablespoons caraway seeds. Cover. Let rise until double in size. Bake in a preheated hot oven, 400°F for about 15 minutes. YIELD: 24 party-size rolls.

  * See pp 20–21 for alternative to hot roll mix.

Tiny Herb Loaves

Milk	½ cup
Sugar	3 tablespoons
Salt	2 teaspoons
Margarine	3 tablespoons
Warm water	1½ cups
Active dry yeast *or*	1 package
Compressed yeast	1 cake
Unsifted flour	5½–6½ cups
Chives, chopped	1 cup
Parsley, chopped	1 cup
Margarine, melted for brushing	

Scald milk; stir in sugar, salt and margarine. Cool to lukewarm. Measure warm water into large bowl. Sprinkle in yeast: stir until dissolved. Add lukewarm milk mixture and 3 cups or half the flour. Beat until smooth. Stir in enough of the additional flour to form a stiff dough. Turn out on to lightly floured board; knead until smooth and elastic, about 8 to 10 minutes. Place in greased bowl, turning to grease top. Cover; let rise in warm place, free from draught, until doubled in bulk, about 1 hour. Combine chives and parsley; toss to blend. Punch down dough: turn out on to board. Cover; let rest 15 minutes. Divide dough into 6 equal pieces. Roll each piece into a rectangle, 12 × 8in. Brush with melted margarine. Sprinkle with chive-parsley mixture. Roll up tightly in 12in rolls; pinch seams to seal. Place on greased baking sheets 2in apart. Cover; let rise in warm place, free from draught, until doubled in bulk, about 1 hour. Bake at 375°F (moderate oven) for 15 to 20 minutes or until done. YIELD: 6 small loaves.

Orange Spice Bread

Sugar	1 cup
Soft butter *or*	
margarine	$\frac{1}{3}$ cup
Grated orange rind	1 tablespoon
Eggs	2
Unsifted all-purpose	
flour	$2\frac{3}{4}$ cups
Wheat germ	$\frac{1}{2}$ cup
Cardamom, ground	2 tablespoons
Cinnamon, ground	2 tablespoons
Baking powder	3 teaspoons
Baking soda	$\frac{1}{2}$ teaspoon
Salt	1 teaspoon
Orange juice	1 cup
Pecans, chopped	$\frac{1}{2}$ cup

Cream sugar, butter and orange rind thoroughly. Add eggs one at a time, mixing well after each addition. Measure dry ingredients, including spices, to creamed mixture alternately with orange juice. Stir until all ingredients are moistened. Stir in pecans. Pour into well-greased 9 × 5 × 3in loaf pan. Bake at 350°F (moderate oven) for 55 to 60 minutes or until toothpick inserted in centre comes out clean. Remove from pan immediately. Cool on rack. YIELD: 1 large loaf.

Spicy Date Muffins

Unsifted all-purpose	
flour	$1\frac{1}{2}$ cups
Wheat germ	$\frac{1}{3}$ cup
Cardamom, ground	2 tablespoons
Anise seeds	1 tablespoon
Fennel seeds	1 teaspoon
Sugar	$\frac{1}{3}$ cup
Baking powder	3 teaspoons
Salt	$\frac{1}{2}$ teaspoon

Dates, chopped	1 cup
Milk	⅔ cup
Cooking oil *or*	
melted shortening	¼ cup
Eggs	2

Measure all dry ingredients, and spices, into bowl. Stir well to blend. Stir in dates. Combine milk, oil and eggs in small bowl. Beat slightly. Add liquid ingredients to blended dry ingredients all at once. Stir with fork just until all ingredients are moistened. Fill paper-lined muffin pans ⅔ full. Bake at 400°F (hot oven) for 18 to 20 minutes. Serve warm with butter. YIELD: 12 muffins.

Banana Herb Muffins

Unsifted all-purpose	
flour	1½ cups
Wheat germ	1 cup
Poppy seeds	1 tablespoon
Sesame seeds	1 tablespoon
Saffron, powdered	¼ teaspoon
Sugar	½ cup
Baking powder	3 teaspoons
Salt	½ teaspoon
Bananas, mashed	1 cup (about 3 bananas)
Milk	½ cup
Cooking oil *or* melted	
shortening	¼ cup
Eggs	2

Measure all dry ingredients into bowl. Stir well to blend. Combine banana, milk, oil and eggs in small bowl. Beat slightly. Add liquid ingredients to blended dry ingredients all at once. Stir just until all ingredients are moistened. Fill well-greased or paper-lined muffin pans ⅔ full. Bake at 400°F (hot oven) for 20 to 25 minutes. Serve warm with butter. YIELD: 12 large muffins.

Spice Flavored Pancakes

Unsifted all-purpose flour	1 cup
Wheat germ	½ cup
Cinnamon	1 teaspoon
Ginger	½ teaspoon
Nutmeg	¼ teaspoon
Baking powder	1 teaspoon
Salt	½ teaspoon
Milk	1½ cups
Bananas, mashed	½ cup (1–2 bananas)
Eggs	2

Measure all dry ingredients into bowl. Stir well to blend. Add remaining ingredients. Beat with rotary beater until well blended. Pour batter by ¼ cupfuls on to lightly greased hot griddle. Bake until puffy and bubbly. Turn and bake other side. Serve hot with butter and syrup. YIELD: 12 (5in) pancakes.

Spice Biscuits (Scones)

Unsifted all-purpose flour	1½ cups
Wheat germ	½ cup
Cinnamon, ground	2 teaspoons
Sesame seeds	1 teaspoon
Saffron, powdered	¼ teaspoon
Baking powder	3 teaspoons
Salt	1 teaspoon
Shortening	¼ cup
Milk	¾ cup

Measure all dry ingredients into a bowl. Stir well to blend. Cut in shortening with pastry blender or rub in with fingers until mixture resembles coarse meal. Add milk. Stir with fork until all ingredients are moistened. Turn out on to lightly floured, cloth-covered board. Knead gently 20 times. Roll dough to ½in thickness. Cut with floured 2in biscuit cutter—one sharp cut for each. Place on ungreased baking sheet. Bake at 450°F (very hot oven) for 8 to 10 minutes. YIELD: 12 biscuits.

Spice Waffles

Unsifted all-purpose flour	1¾ cups
Wheat germ	⅔ cup
Ginger, ground	1 teaspoon
Nutmeg, grated	½ teaspoon
Cinnamon, ground	½ teaspoon
Sugar	3 tablespoons
Baking powder	2 teaspoons
Salt	½ teaspoon
Milk	2 cups
Cooking oil *or* melted shortening	⅓ cup
Eggs, separated	2

Measure flour, wheat germ, spices, sugar, baking powder and salt into bowl. Stir well to blend. Combine milk, oil and egg yolks in small bowl. Beat well. Add liquid ingredients to blended dry ingredients. Beat until smooth. Fold in stiffly beaten egg whites. Bake in preheated waffle iron until golden brown (about 5 minutes). YIELD: 4 (9in) square waffles.

Clove-Kissed Gingerbread

Unsifted all-purpose flour	2 cups
Wheat germ	½ cup
Sugar	½ cup
Baking soda	1 teaspoon
Salt	¾ teaspoon
Cinnamon, ground	1½ teaspoons
Ginger, ground	1½ teaspoons
Cloves, ground	¼ teaspoon

Buttermilk	1 cup
Light molasses	¾ cup
Cooking oil *or*	
melted shortening	⅓ cup

Measure dry ingredients into bowl. Stir well to blend. Add liquid ingredients to blended dry ingredients. Mix well. Pour into well-greased 9in square pan. Bake at 350°F (moderate oven) for 35 to 40 minutes. Cool on rack 5 minutes before removing from pan. TIP: Serve with lemon sauce or whipped cream. YIELD: Serves 9.

Simple Spice Bread

Sifted all-purpose	
flour	2 cups
Salt	½ teaspoon
Baking powder	3 teaspoons
Caraway seeds	2 tablespoons
Cinnamon, ground	1 tablespoon
Ginger, ground	½ teaspoon
Saffron, powdered	¼ teaspoon
Sugar	½ cup
Nuts, chopped	½ cup
Eggs	1
Milk	1 cup
Bananas, mashed	1 cup (3 bananas)

Sift into bowl flour, salt, baking powder, spices, sugar. Add chopped nuts. In small bowl, beat egg with fork. Add milk, mashed bananas. Add liquid ingredients to dry ingredients. Stir gently until dry ingredients are moist. (Careful . . . don't over-stir.) Pour batter into lightly greased loaf pan, 3½ × 7½ × 3in. Bake at 350°F (moderate oven) for 1 hour. Cool on rack. YIELD: 1 large loaf.

Spice Yeast Bread

Warm water	1¼ cups
Active dry yeast *or*	1 package
Compressed yeast	1 cake
Poppy seeds	1 tablespoon
Sesame seeds	1 tablespoon
Cinnamon, ground	1 teaspoon
Anise seeds	¼ teaspoon
Soft margarine *or* shortening	2 tablespoons
Sugar	2 tablespoons
Salt	2 teaspoons
Sifted all-purpose flour	3 cups

Measure warm water into large mixer bowl. Sprinkle in yeast: stir until dissolved. Add margarine, sugar, salt and 2 cups of flour. Beat 2 minutes at medium speed on mixer or 300 vigorous strokes by hand. Scrape sides and bottom of bowl frequently. Blend in remaining flour and all spices with spoon until smooth. Cover; let rise in warm place, free from draught, until doubled in bulk, about 30 minutes. Stir batter down by beating about 25 strokes. Spread evenly in greased 9 × 5 × 3in loaf pan. Smooth loaf by flouring your hand and patting top into shape. Cover; let rise until doubled, about 40 minutes. Bake at 375°F (moderate) for about 45 minutes or until loaf sounds hollow when tapped. YIELD: 1 loaf.

Whole Wheat Yeast Spice Bread

Active dry yeast *or*	2 packages
Compressed yeast	2 cakes
Warm water	½ cup
Poppy seeds	1 tablespoon
Cardamom, ground	1 teaspoon
Nutmeg, ground	1 teaspoon

Warm milk	1 cup
Sugar	1 tablespoon
Salt	2 teaspoons
Molasses	¼ cup
Shortening	1 tablespoon
Sifted all-purpose flour	2 cups
Whole wheat flour	3 cups

In mixing bowl, dissolve yeast in warm water. Blend in poppy seeds, cardamom, nutmeg, milk, sugar, salt and molasses. Mix in shortening and flour with spoon. Mix in whole wheat flour with hand. Turn on to lightly floured board; knead until smooth, 5 to 10 minutes. Round up in greased bowl; let rise until double, 50 to 60 minutes. Shape into a loaf to fit a greased 9 × 5 × 3in pan. Let rise again until amost double. Heat oven to 400°F (hot oven). Bake 30 to 35 minutes. YIELD: 1 large loaf.

14

Wine Flavored Breads

Baking with wine will give bread a unique, piquant flavor to please all appetites. Wine can be used modestly to enhance and bring out the many hidden flavors in most bread recipes.

Orange Sherry Muffins

Sifted all-purpose flour	2 cups
Sugar	$\frac{1}{3}$ cup
Baking powder	3 teaspoons
Salt	1 teaspoon
Mace, ground	$\frac{1}{4}$ teaspoon
Walnuts, chopped	$\frac{1}{2}$ cup
Eggs	1
Grated orange rind	1 tablespoon
Milk	$\frac{2}{3}$ cup
California sherry	$\frac{1}{3}$ cup
Shortening, melted	$\frac{1}{4}$ cup

Sift flour with sugar, baking powder, salt and mace. Add walnuts. Beat egg lightly, add orange rind, milk, sherry and shortening. Stir into dry mixture, blending only until all of flour is moistened. Spoon into greased muffin pans. Bake at 425°F (hot oven) for about 20 minutes. Serve hot. YIELD: 12.

Cheddar Onion Wine Muffins

Biscuit mix*	2 cups
Cheddar cheese, grated	1 cup

Green onion, finely chopped	⅓ cup
Salt	¼ teaspoon
California sauterne *or* other white dinner wine	¼ cup
Eggs, beaten	1
Milk	½ cup

Combine biscuit mix, cheese, onion and salt. Stir in wine, egg and milk. Spoon into greased muffin cups, filling about ⅔ full. Bake at 400°F (hot oven) for 15 to 20 minutes. Serve hot. YIELD: 12.

* See pp 19–20 for alternatives to biscuit mix.

Chili Onion Wine Corn Sticks

Yellow cornmeal	1 cup
Sifted all-purpose flour	1 cup
Baking powder	2 teaspoons
Salt	1 teaspoon
Sugar	1 tablespoon
Chili powder	¼ teaspoon
Shortening	⅓ cup
California sauterne *or* other white dinner wine	¾ cup
Onion, finely chopped	1 tablespoon
Eggs, beaten	1
Milk	½ cup

Sift cornmeal, flour, baking powder, salt, sugar and chili powder together into a mixing bowl. Cut in shortening until in small pieces. Stir in wine and onion; add egg and milk and stir until blended. Spoon into well-greased corn stick pans, filling pans about ⅔ full. Bake at 400°F (hot oven) for about 15 minutes or until baked and crusty. YIELD: 12 to 14 corn sticks.

Orange Fig Muffins with Sherry Fig Filling

Biscuit mix*	2 cups
Sugar	¼ cup
Butter *or* margarine, melted	2 tablespoons
Grated orange rind	¼ teaspoon
Orange juice	¼ cup
Eggs, beaten	1
Milk	½ cup
Sherry Fig Filling:	
Dried golden figs, chopped finely	1½ cups
California sherry	1 cup
Grated orange rind	½ teaspoon
Salt	¼ teaspoon
Sugar	¼ cup

Sherry Fig Filling: Combine the finely chopped dried golden figs, California sherry, grated orange rind, and salt in a saucepan. Bring to boil, lower heat and simmer 5 minutes. Add the sugar and cook 3 to 4 minutes longer or until thickened, stirring now and then. Remove from heat and cool.

Measure biscuit mix and sugar into mixing bowl. Make a well in center and add butter, orange rind and juice, egg and milk. Stir just until blended. Spoon into greased muffin cups (about 2in diameter), filling pans about ½ full. Spoon a generous tablespoon sherry fig filling in center of each, pressing down slightly. Bake at 400°F (hot oven) for 15 to 20 minutes. Serve hot. YIELD: About 18.

* See pp 19–20 for alternatives to biscuit mix.

Sherry Orange Muffins

Eggs	1
Sugar	¼ cup
California sherry	½ cup

Soft shortening	2 tablespoons
Packaged biscuit mix*	2 cups
Orange marmalade	$\frac{1}{2}$ cup
Pecans, chopped	$\frac{1}{2}$ cup
Spicy Topping:	
Sugar	$\frac{1}{4}$ cup
Flour	$1\frac{1}{2}$ tablespoons
Cinnamon	$\frac{1}{2}$ teaspoon
Nutmeg	$\frac{1}{4}$ teaspoon
Butter	1 tablespoon

Spicy Topping: Combine sugar, flour, cinnamon and nutmeg in a small bowl. Cut or rub in the butter until in fine pieces.

Beat egg lightly. Combine with sugar, sherry and shortening. Add biscuit mix and beat 30 seconds. Stir in marmalade and pecans. Spoon into greased muffin pans (or paper baking cups set in muffin tins). Fill pans $\frac{2}{3}$ full of batter. Sprinkle with spicy topping. Bake at 400°F (hot oven) for 20 to 25 minutes. Serve hot. YIELD: 12.

* See pp 19–20 for alternatives to packaged biscuit mix.

Sherry Nut Loaf

Sugar	$\frac{1}{3}$ cup
Eggs	2
Soft shortening	3 tablespoons
Milk	$\frac{3}{4}$ cup
California sherry	$\frac{1}{4}$ cup
Packaged biscuit mix*	$3\frac{1}{2}$ cups
Whole cranberry sauce	1 can (1lb)
Mincemeat	$\frac{1}{3}$ cup
Walnuts, chopped (optional)	$\frac{1}{2}$ cup

Combine sugar, eggs, shortening, milk, wine and biscuit mix in large mixing bowl. Beat vigorously about 30 seconds. Spread dough in greased 13 × 9 × 2in pan. Combine cranberry sauce and mincemeat. Drop by spoonfuls over top of dough. Run spatula or knife in spiral pattern through batter. Sprinkle with chopped walnuts, if desired. Bake at 400°F (hot oven) for 25 to 30 minutes or until loaf tests done. Cut in squares and serve fresh and warm with butter. YIELD: 1 large loaf.

* See pp 19–20 for alternatives to packaged biscuit mix.

Parmesan Wine Bread

Packaged biscuit mix*	2 cups
Sugar	1 tablespoon
Instant minced onion *or*	1 teaspoon
Mild onion, finely chopped	1 tablespoon
Crushed oregano *or*	½ teaspoon
Powdered oregano	¼ teaspoon
Butter *or* margarine, melted	¼ cup
California sauterne, chablis *or* other white dinner wine	¼ cup
Eggs, beaten	1
Milk	½ cup
Parmesan cheese, grated	¼ cup

Combine biscuit mix, sugar, onion and oregano. Add melted butter, wine, beaten egg and milk. Beat until blended. Turn into a well-greased 8in round cake pan. Sprinkle Parmesan cheese over top. Bake at 400°F (hot oven) for 20 to 25 minutes. Serve warm in triangular wedges. YIELD: 1 large loaf.

* See pp 19–20 for alternatives to packaged biscuit mix.

Apple Rolls with Muscatel Sauce

Packaged biscuit mix*	2 cups
Cinnamon	$1\frac{1}{2}$ teaspoons
Milk	$\frac{2}{3}$ cup
Cooking apples, finely chopped	2 cups
Sugar	1 cup
Grated lemon rind	1 teaspoon
Salt	$\frac{1}{4}$ teaspoon
California muscatel	$\frac{1}{4}$ cup
Muscatel Sauce:	
Sugar	$\frac{2}{3}$ cup
Corn starch	2 tablespoons
Salt	$\frac{1}{8}$ teaspoon
Water	$\frac{3}{4}$ cup
California muscatel	$\frac{3}{4}$ cup
Butter	1 tablespoon

Muscatel Sauce: Blend together sugar, corn starch and salt in a saucepan. Stir in water and California muscatel. Cook and stir over moderate heat until sauce is thickened and clear. Add butter, stir until melted. Serve warm over apple rolls.

Stir biscuit mix with $\frac{1}{2}$ teaspoon cinnamon. Add milk, mixing to moderately stiff dough. Roll out on lightly floured board to a rectangle about 10 × 12in. Sprinkle surface with apples, then remaining cinnamon, sugar, lemon rind and salt. Roll up as for jelly roll starting from the long side. Cut into 8 or 9 equal slices. Arrange in a buttered 9in square pan or oblong baking pan with rolls barely touching one another. Sprinkle with muscatel. Bake at 400°F (hot oven) for about 30 minutes or until rolls are a rich crusty brown. Serve warm with muscatel sauce and a topping of whipped cream or vanilla ice cream, if desired. YIELD: Serves 8 or 9.

* See pp 19–20 for alternatives to packaged biscuit mix.

Wine Biscuits-in-the-Round

Packaged biscuit mix*	2 cups
Crushed chervil	½ teaspoon
Crushed sweet basil	¼ teaspoon
Sharp Cheddar cheese, grated	1 cup
California sauterne, chablis *or* other white dinner wine	½ cup
Milk	⅓ cup

Combine biscuit mix, chervil, basil and cheese. Add wine and milk. Stir until dry ingredients are well blended. Drop dough by large spoonfuls into a well-greased, 8in, round layer baking pan (7 portions around outer edge of pan and 1 in center will fit nicely). Bake at 425°F (hot oven) until biscuits are rich golden brown, about 12 to 15 minutes. Serve hot with butter. YIELD: 8 biscuits.

* See pp 19–20 for alternatives to packaged biscuit mix.

Sherry Loaf

Packaged biscuit mix*	4 cups
Light brown sugar	⅓ cup, packed
Cinnamon	1½ teaspoons
Nutmeg, grated	¼ teaspoon
Large eggs, beaten	1
Milk	1 cup
California sherry	¼ cup
Butter, melted	6 tablespoons
Caramel Crunch:	
Light brown sugar	½ cup, packed
Grated lemon rind	1 teaspoon
Walnuts, chopped	⅓ cup
Butter	2 tablespoons

Caramel Crunch: Measure light brown sugar (packed), grated lemon rind, chopped walnuts and butter into small mixing bowl. Mix together until crumbly.

Measure biscuit mix into a bowl. Blend in brown sugar and spices. Add beaten egg, milk, sherry and 4 tablespoons butter. Beat until well blended and smooth. Turn half the batter into well-buttered, 9in square pan or any similar pan of 5 to 6 cup capacity. Drizzle remaining butter over top; sprinkle on half of caramel crunch. Carefully cover with remaining batter, sprinkle with remaining caramel crunch. Bake at 350°F (moderate oven) for 30 to 35 minutes or until loaf is done. Let stand in pan 5 minutes before removing. Serve warm or cold. YIELD: Serves 8.

* See pp 19–20 for alternatives to packaged biscuit mix.

Peanut Butter Wine Bread

California sherry	$\frac{1}{3}$ cup
Peanut butter	$\frac{2}{3}$ cup
Sugar	1 cup
Soft shortening	1 tablespoon
Eggs	1
Milk	$\frac{2}{3}$ cup
Sifted all-purpose flour	2 cups
Baking powder	$3\frac{1}{2}$ teaspoons
Salt	$\frac{3}{4}$ teaspoon
Peanuts, chopped	$\frac{1}{2}$ cup

Beat sherry, peanut butter, sugar, shortening, egg and milk together until thoroughly blended and smooth. Resift flour with baking powder and salt. Add to first mixture, blending just until smooth; stir in peanuts. Spoon into a well-greased loaf pan, $8\frac{1}{2} \times 4\frac{1}{2} \times 2\frac{3}{4}$in. Let stand 20 minutes, then bake at 350°F (moderate oven) for 1 hour and 15 minutes or just until loaf is done. Turn out on wire rack; cool thoroughly before storing. YIELD: 1 loaf.

Golden Gate Wine Bread

California sherry	$\frac{3}{4}$ cup
Baking soda	1 teaspoon
Pitted dates chopped	1 cup
Shortening	$\frac{1}{4}$ cup
Sugar	1 cup
Eggs, beaten	2
Vanilla	1 teaspoon
Sifted all-purpose flour	2 cups
Double acting baking powder	1 teaspoon
Salt	$\frac{1}{2}$ teaspoon
Walnuts, chopped	$\frac{1}{2}$ cup

Heat sherry to just below boiling. Sprinkle baking soda over dates in a bowl. Pour over hot sherry; cool. Cream together shortening and sugar. Add cooled sherry-date mixture, beaten eggs and vanilla; mix well. Sift flour with baking powder and salt; add to creamed mixture, stirring till blended. Stir in nuts. Pour into 2 greased ($7\frac{1}{2} \times 4 \times 2\frac{1}{2}$in) loaf pans or 1 ($8\frac{1}{2} \times 4\frac{1}{2} \times$ 3in) loaf pan. Bake at 350°F (moderate oven) for 50 to 60 minutes. YIELD: 1 large loaf or 2 small loaves.

Holiday Brunch Wine Muffins

Large eggs	1
Butter *or* margarine, melted	$\frac{1}{4}$ cup
California sherry	$\frac{1}{4}$ cup
Sugar	$\frac{1}{3}$ cup
Sifted all-purpose flour	1 cup
Baking powder	$2\frac{1}{2}$ teaspoons
Salt	1 teaspoon
Bran flakes	1 cup
Pecans, chopped	$\frac{1}{4}$ cup
Raisins, chopped	$\frac{1}{4}$ cup

Beat egg well. Add butter, sherry and sugar. Resift flour with baking powder and salt into egg mixture. Add bran flakes. Stir slowly just until ingredients are blended. Gently fold in pecans and raisins. Spoon into well-greased, medium-sized muffin pans; fill pans about ¾ full. Bake at 400°F (hot oven) for 15 to 20 minutes until muffins are done and a rich golden brown. Serve hot. TIP: Each muffin may be topped with a pecan-half before baking, if desired. YIELD: 8 medium-size muffins.

Festive Breads

No matter what the holiday or occasion, bread can be used as part of the celebration. The addition of special fruits, herbs, and wines, can turn simple breads into 'party time' main courses.

Confetti Loaf

Butter *or* margarine	½ cup
Sugar	1 cup
Eggs	2
Sifted all-purpose flour	2 cups
Baking powder	1½ teaspoons
Salt	½ teaspoon
Baking soda	1½ teaspoon
Banana pulp	1½ cups (4 bananas)
Fresh apple, grated	½ cup
Red maraschino cherries	6
Green maraschino cherries	6
Hickory nuts (*or* pecans), chopped	1 cup
Orange juice	2 tablespoons

Cream butter and sugar; add eggs and beat until light and fluffy. Sift together dry ingredients. Add alternately with banana pulp to creamed mixture. Blend well. Add apple, cherries, nuts and orange juice. Mix well. Spoon into two small greased and floured loaf pans. Bake at 350°F (moderate oven) for 1 hour. Cool 5 minutes before removing from pan. YIELD: 2 small loaves.

Hush Puppies

Cornmeal	1½ cups
Water	1½ cups
Milk	⅓ cup
Salad oil	1 tablespoon
Onion, grated	2 teaspoons
Eggs, beaten	2
Sifted all-purpose flour	1 cup
Baking powder	3 teaspoons
Salt	2 teaspoons
Sugar	1 teaspoon

Cook and stir cornmeal and water until mixture becomes stiff and begins to form a ball, about 6 minutes. Remove from heat; add milk, oil and onion. Stir until smooth. Gradually stir into eggs in medium bowl. Stir dry ingredients together. Add to cornmeal mixture; blend thoroughly. Heat oil (1in deep) to 375°F. Drop batter by teaspoonfuls into hot oil. Fry 6 to 7 minutes or until golden brown. Drain on paper towels. YIELD: From 24 to 30.

Dumplings Delight

Sifted all-purpose flour	1½ cups
Baking powder	2 teaspoons
Salt	¾ teaspoon
Shortening	3 tablespoons
Milk	¾ cup

Measure flour, baking powder and salt into mixing bowl. Cut or rub in shortening until mixture looks like meal. Blend in milk. Drop dough by spoonfuls on to hot meal or vegetables in boiling stew. (Do not drop directly into liquid.) Cook uncovered 10 minutes; cover and cook 10 minutes longer. YIELD: 8 to 10.

Basic Bagel

Warm water	
(105–15°F)	1½ cups
Active dry yeast *or*	1 package
Compressed yeast	1 cake
Sugar	3 tablespoons
Salt	1 tablespoon
Unsifted flour	4¼ cups

Rinse a large bowl under hot water (to warm bowl). Pour in the warm water. Sprinkle or crumble yeast on top; stir till dissolved. Stir in sugar, salt and enough flour to make a soft dough. Turn out on to lightly floured board and knead about 10 minutes (adding flour to board as needed) until dough is smooth and elastic. Cover; let rise in a warm place, free from draughts, for 15 minutes. Punch down dough and roll on lightly floured board into a rectangle about 5 × 9in. Dough should be 1in thick. Cut it into 12 equal strips with a floured knife. Roll each strip till it is only ½in thick; moisten ends and join together to form bagels. Cover; let rise in a warm place again for about 20 minutes. Bring 1 gallon (4 quarts) of water to the boil, lower heat and add 4 or 5 bagels. Simmer them exactly 7 minutes (longer will cause sogginess). Remove and cool on a towel while you cook remaining bagels. Bake on ungreased cookie sheet at 375°F (moderate oven) for 30 to 35 minutes. Cool and eat—or wrap and freeze. YIELD: one dozen.

Honey Nut Swirls

Prepared biscuit mix*	2 cups
Butter	¼ cup
Honey	2 tablespoons
Milk	½ cup

Measure biscuit mix; cut or rub in soft butter. Combine honey and milk; add to mix, stirring until you have a soft dough. Roll out on floured board to a 10 × 14in rectangle.

Spread half of the honey-butter mixture (see below) over dough.
Roll up dough into long roll. Using sharp knife, cut into 16 slices.
Place in 8 × 8 × 2in buttered pan. Spread balance of honey-
butter mixture lightly over top of rolls. Bake at 400°F (hot oven)
15 to 20 minutes or until done. Serve piping hot. YIELD: 16 rolls.

SUGGESTION: *Honey-Butter Topping and Filling:* Cream together ½ cup honey, ¼ cup soft butter; add ½ cup finely chopped
walnuts. Use as topping and filling.

* See pp 19–20 for alternatives to prepared biscuit mix.

Stollen

Active dry yeast *or*	1 package
Compressed yeast	1 cake
Warm water	¼ cup
Milk	⅔ cup
Butter *or* margarine	½ cup
Sugar	¼ cup
Eggs	1
Almond extract	½ teaspoon
Salt	½ teaspoon
Sifted all-purpose flour	3¼–3½ cups
Almonds, blanched and slivered	¾ cup
Golden raisins	1 cup
Candied cherries, halved	½ cup

Confectioners' sugar icing for spreading on top of baked loaf

Dissolve yeast in water. Scald milk; add butter and sugar
and stir until sugar is dissolved. Cool to lukewarm. Beat egg
and add to milk mixture with yeast, almond extract and salt.
Stir in 2 cups flour and beat until smooth. Stir in almonds,
raisins and cherries. Add remaining flour, and mix to form
smooth dough. Cover and let rise in warm place until doubled in
bulk (about 1½ hours). Punch down; knead lightly and pat to
12in circle. Fold in half, and press edges together firmly. Place on

greased baking sheet. Brush top with melted butter. Let rise ½ hour in warm place. Bake at 350°F (moderate oven) for about 30 minutes. Spread top with icing while warm. YIELD: 1 large loaf.

Holiday Berry Nut Bread

Sifted all-purpose flour	2 cups
Sugar	1 cup
Double acting baking powder	1½ teaspoons
Baking soda	½ teaspoon
Salt	1 teaspoon
Shortening	¼ cup
Orange juice	¾ cup
Grated orange rind	1 tablespoon
Eggs, well-beaten	1
Nuts, chopped	½ cup
Fresh *or* frozen cranberries, coarsely chopped	1 or 2 cups

Sift together flour, sugar, baking powder, soda and salt. Cut or rub in shortening until mixture resembles coarse cornmeal. Combine orange juice and grated rind with well-beaten egg. Pour all at once into dry ingredients, mixing just enough to dampen. Carefully fold in chopped nuts and berries. Spoon into greased loaf pan, 9 × 5 × 3in. Spread corners and sides slightly higher than center. Bake at 350°F (moderate oven) for about 1 hour or until crust is golden brown and inserted toothpick comes out clean. Remove from pan. Cool. Store overnight for easy slicing. YIELD: 1 large festive loaf.

NOTE: If frozen cranberries are used, do not thaw. Give them a quick rinse in cold water and chop while frozen.

Spicy Tea Ring

Active dry yeast *or*	1 package
Compressed yeast	1 cake
Warm milk (110°F)	1 cup
Sugar	2 tablespoons
Sifted all-purpose flour	3 cups
Salt	1 teaspoon
Butter *or* margarine	3 tablespoons
Melted butter	1 tablespoon
Brown sugar	4 tablespoons
Cinnamon	2 teaspoons
Confectioners' sugar frosting	
Candied cherries, chopped	for decoration
Nuts, chopped	

Sprinkle or crumble the yeast onto the warm milk in which 1 teaspoon sugar has been dissolved. Stir the compressed yeast to dissolve, allow the dried yeast to stand for 10 minutes until frothy. Sift flour, salt and sugar into a mixing bowl. Cut or rub in butter or margarine. Add dissolved or reconstituted yeast and mix to form a firm dough, adding extra flour if needed. Turn dough on to a lightly floured board and knead until smooth, 10 minutes. Place in a greased bowl and turn to grease the top. Cover and let rise until double in size, about 1 hour in a warm place. Turn out on to a lightly floured board and roll to a rectangle 9 × 12in. Brush lightly with melted butter and sprinkle the brown sugar and cinnamon mixed together over the dough. Roll up tightly from the long edge and seal the ends together to form a ring. Place on a greased baking sheet, seam side downwards and with scissors cut slashes at an angle 1in apart to within ½in of the center. Turn the cut sections on their sides. Cover and let rise until doubled in bulk, about 30 minutes. Bake at 375°F (moderate oven) for 30 to 35 minutes. Cool on a wire rack then decorate with confectioners' frosting, chopped cherries and nuts. YIELD: 1 large ring.

Holiday Cheese Tempters

Soft sharp cheese spread	1½ cups
Soft margarine *or* butter	¼ cup
Packaged baking mix*	¾ cup
Salt	¼ teaspoon
Cornflakes	1 cup
Paprika for sprinkling	

Heat oven to 400°F (hot oven). Combine cheese and margarine or butter, add baking mix and salt. Blend in thoroughly. Stir in cornflakes. Drop dough by teaspoon on to ungreased baking sheets. Sprinkle with paprika. Bake 6 to 8 minutes. YIELD: About 36 tempters.

* See pp 19–20 for alternatives to packaged baking mix.

Nutty Pizza

Packaged baking mix*	2 cups
Sugar	2 tablespoons
Milk	⅓ cup
Margarine *or* butter, melted	½ cup
Brown sugar	¼ cup, packed
Light corn syrup	⅓ cup
Nuts, chopped	½ cup

Heat oven to 450°F (very hot oven). Combine baking mix sugar, milk and ½ of the melted butter, until blended. Pat into 13in pizza pan. Mix remaining melted butter, sugar, syrup and nuts and spread this mixture over dough. Bake for about 10 minutes. Cut into wedges and serve warm. YIELD: 10 servings.

* See pp 19–20 for alternatives to packaged baking mix.

Yuletide Fruitbread

Packaged honey date muffin mix	1 package
Eggs	1
Milk	¼ cup
Dried apricots *or*	2 cups
Candied pineapple, cut up	2 cups
Brazil nuts *or* walnuts	1½ cups
Drained red maraschino cherries	½ cup
Drained green maraschino cherries	½ cup

Preheat oven to 300°F (slow oven). Grease loaf pan, 9 × 5in. Mix muffin mix, eggs and milk together. Leave apricots, nuts and cherries whole and stir into batter with remaining ingredients. Pour into prepared pan. Bake about 1 hour and 20 minutes. YIELD: 1 loaf.

Festive Nut Bread

All-purpose butter-milk biscuit mix*	3 cups
Sugar	⅔ cup
Sifted all-purpose flour	¼ cup
Eggs	1
Orange juice	1 cup
Dried apricots, cut up	1 cup
Nuts, chopped	¾ cup

Preheat oven to 350°F (moderate oven). Meanwhile, combine baking mix, sugar, flour, egg and orange juice; beat vigorously

½ minute. Stir in apricots and nuts. Pour batter into greased loaf pan, 9 × 5 × 3in. Bake up to 60 minutes or until wooden pick inserted in centre comes out clean. Cool thoroughly before slicing. YIELD: 1 loaf.

* See p 20 for alternatives to all-purpose buttermilk biscuit mix.

No-Sift Cherry Nut Bread

Sugar	1 cup
Shortening	½ cup
Eggs	2
Sifted all-purpose flour	2¼ cups
Salt	½ teaspoon
Milk	½ cup
Maraschino cherry juice	¼ cup
Pecans *or* walnuts, chopped	¾ cup
Maraschino cherries cut up	⅓ cup

Cream sugar, shortening and eggs until light. Spoon flour (not sifted) into dry measuring cup. Level off and pour measured flour on to wax paper. Add baking powder and salt to flour (not sifted). Stir to blend. Add blended dry ingredients to creamed mixture alternately with milk and cherry juice. Stir until all ingredients are moistened. Stir in nuts and cherries. Spread in well-greased 9 × 5 × 3in loaf pan. Bake at 350°F (moderate oven) for 60 to 65 minutes or until toothpick inserted in centre comes out clean. Remove from pan immediately. Cool on rack. YIELD: 1 large loaf.

No-Sift Lemon Nut Bread

Sugar	¾ cup
Soft butter	3 tablespoons
Eggs	2
Sifted all-purpose flour	2 cups

Baking powder	3 teaspoons
Salt	1 teaspoon
Milk	1 cup
Walnuts, chopped	1 cup
Grated lemon rind	3 tablespoons

Cream sugar, butter and eggs until light. Spoon flour (not sifted) into dry measuring cup. Level off and pour measured flour on to wax paper. Add baking powder and salt to flour (not sifted). Stir to blend. Add blended dry ingredients to creamed mixture alternately with milk. Stir until all ingredients are moistened. Stir in nuts and lemon rind. Spread in well-greased 9 × 5 × 3in loaf pan. Cover and let stand 20 minutes. Bake at 350°F (moderate oven) for 55 to 60 minutes or until toothpick inserted in centre comes out clean. Remove from pan immediately. Cool on rack. YIELD: 1 large loaf.

No-Sift Apple Crisp

Apples, peeled and sliced	6 cups (4 large apples)
Water	½ cup
Lemon juice	2 teaspoons
Sifted all-purpose flour	¾ cup
Brown sugar	½ cup, packed
Granulated sugar	½ cup
Cinnamon	1 teaspoon
Butter	½ cup

Arrange prepared apples in well-greased 9in square pan or well-greased 2 quart casserole. Sprinkle with water and lemon juice. Spoon flour (not sifted) into dry measuring cup. Level off and pour measured flour into bowl. Add sugars and cinnamon to flour (not sifted). Stir well to blend. Cut in butter with pastry blender or rub in until mixture resembles coarse meal. Spoon crumb mixture evenly over apples. Bake at 375°F (moderate) for 40 to 50 minutes. Serve warm or cold with whipped cream, if desired. YIELD: 9 servings.

Anadama Bread

Unsifted flour	7–8 cups
Yellow cornmeal	1¼ cups
Salt	2½ teaspoons
Active dry yeast *or*	2 packages
Compressed yeast	2 cakes
Soft margarine	⅓ cup
Warm water (120–30°F)	2¼ cups
Molasses	⅔ cup

In a large bowl, thoroughly mix 3 cups flour, cornmeal, salt and undissolved yeast. Add margarine. Gradually add warm water and molasses to dry ingredients and beat 2 minutes at medium speed of electric mixer, scraping bowl occasionally. Add ½ cup flour. Beat at high speed 2 minutes, scraping bowl occasionally. Stir in enough of the additional flour to make a stiff dough. Turn out on to lightly floured board; knead until smooth and elastic, about 8 to 10 minutes. Place in greased bowl, turning to grease top. Cover; let rise in warm place, free from draught, until doubled in bulk, about 1 hour. Punch dough down; divide in half. Roll each half to a 14 × 9in rectangle. Shape into loaves. Place in 2 greased 9 × 5 × 3in loaf pans. Cover; let rise in warm place, free from draught, until doubled in bulk, about 45 minutes. Bake at 375°F (moderate) for about 45 minutes, or until done. Remove from pans and cool on wire racks. YIELD: 2 loaves.

No-Sift Hawaiian Fruit Bread

Sifted all-purpose flour	1¾ cups + 2 teaspoons
Sugar	¼ cup
Baking powder	3 teaspoons
Salt	1 teaspoon
Shortening	¼ cup
Eggs, beaten	1

Pineapple juice ½ cup
Crushed pineapple,
    drained ½ cup

Spoon flour (not sifted) into dry measuring cup. Level off and pour measured flour into bowl. Add sugar, baking powder and salt to flour (not sifted). Stir well to blend. Cut in shortening with pastry blender or rub in until mixture resembles coarse meal. Combine egg, pineapple juice and pineapple in small bowl. Add liquid ingredients to blended dry ingredients. Stir with fork until all ingredients are moistened. Spread in well-greased 8in layer pan. Bake at 425°F (hot oven) for 20 to 25 minutes. Serve warm with sweetened canned or fresh fruit and whipped cream. YIELD: 1 large loaf.

Scotch Scones

Sifted all-purpose flour	2 cups
Sugar	¼ cup
Baking powder	3 teaspoons
Salt	1 teaspoon
Shortening	⅓ cup
Milk	½ cup
Eggs	2
Currants	¼ cup
Granulated sugar for sprinkling	

Spoon flour (not sifted) into dry measuring cup. Level off and pour measured flour into bowl. Add sugar, baking powder and salt to flour (not sifted). Stir well to blend. Cut in shortening with pastry blender or rub in until mixture resembles coarse meal. Add currants, 1 whole egg plus 1 egg yolk and enough milk to give a fairly soft dough when stirred with a fork. Reserve 1 egg white for topping. Beat slightly. Set aside. Now turn out dough on to lightly floured board. Knead gently 20 times. Roll dough into a circle, ½in thick. Brush with beaten egg white. Sprinkle with sugar. Cut into 12 triangular pieces. Place on ungreased baking sheet. Bake at 425°F (hot oven) for 12 to 15 minutes. Serve hot with butter. YIELD: 12 scones.

INDEX

75 76 77 10 9 8 7 6 5 4 3 2